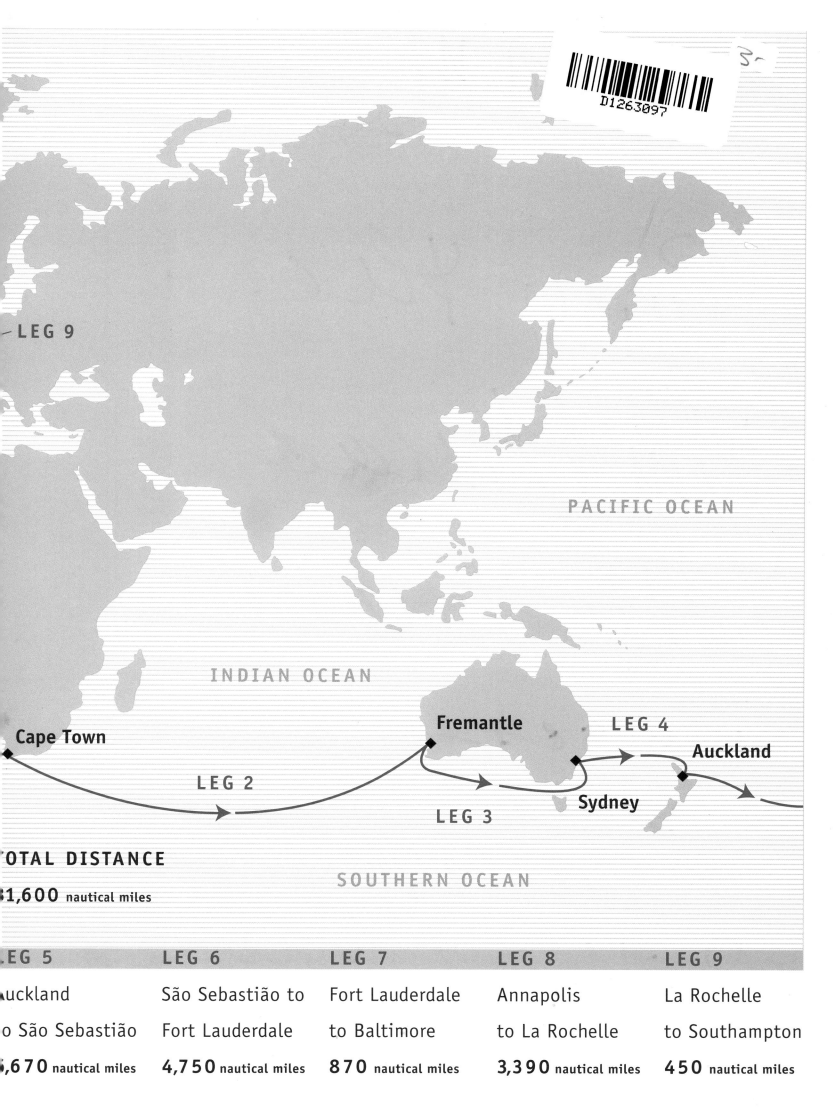

LEG 9

PACIFIC OCEAN

INDIAN OCEAN

Fremantle

LEG 4

Cape Town

Auckland

LEG 2

Sydney

LEG 3

OTAL DISTANCE

SOUTHERN OCEAN

1,600 nautical miles

LEG 5	LEG 6	LEG 7	LEG 8	LEG 9
uckland	São Sebastião to	Fort Lauderdale	Annapolis	La Rochelle
o São Sebastião	Fort Lauderdale	to Baltimore	to La Rochelle	to Southampton
,670 nautical miles	**4,750** nautical miles	**870** nautical miles	**3,390** nautical miles	**450** nautical miles

To Dan M_____

Enjoy the
Whitbread
thru these
pages —
Happy
Sailing
6/25/10

CHESSIE RACING

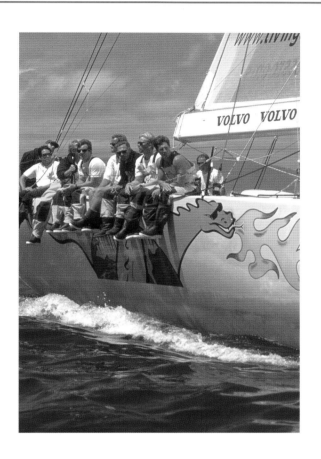

RACING

The Story of Maryland's Entry
in the 1997–1998 Whitbread
Round the World Race

GEORGE J. COLLINS AND

KATHY ALEXANDER

With a foreword by Gary Jobson

THE JOHNS HOPKINS UNIVERSITY PRESS

Baltimore and London

Unless noted otherwise, photographs are by a *Chessie Racing* crew cameraman (Kathy Alexander, Maureen Collins, Rich Deppe, Mark Fischer, Greg Gendell, Pam Gendell, Kurt Lowman, Tony Rey, or Jonathan Swain).

The Johns Hopkins University Press
2715 North Charles Street
Baltimore, Maryland 21218-4363
www.press.jhu.edu

Library of Congress Cataloging-in-Publication Data
Collins, George J., 1940–
    Chessie racing : the story of Maryland's entry in the 1997–1998 Whitbread Round the World Race / George J. Collins and Kathy Alexander; with a fore-word by Gary Jobson.
        p.   cm.
    Includes index.
    ISBN 0-8018-6413-5 (alk. paper)
    1. Chessie (Yacht). 2. Whitbread Round the World Race (7th : 1997–1998). 3. Yacht racing—Maryland—History. I. Alexander, Kathy, 1952– . II. Title.
GV822.C43 C64   2001
797.1'4—dc21   00-008232

A catalog record for this book is available from the British Library.

To the many volunteers who gave selflessly of themselves
and the multitude of students and fans who followed and supported
Chessie Racing *during the Whitbread Round the World Race*

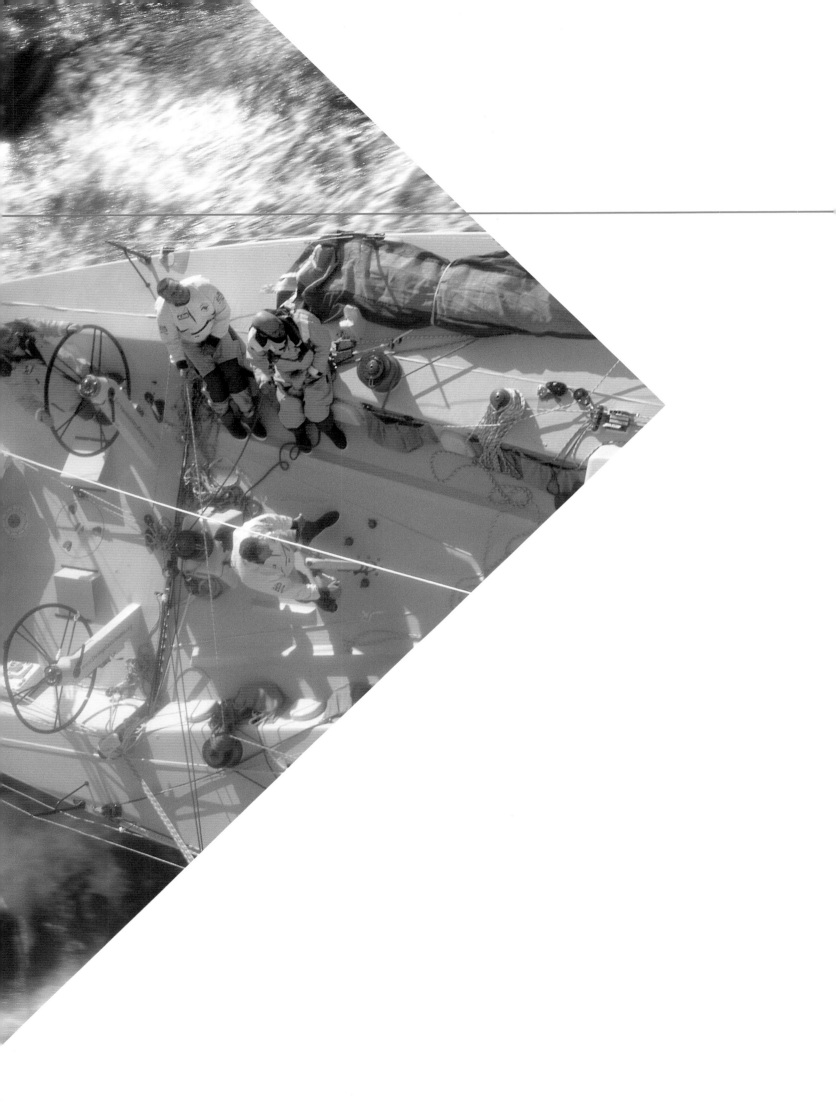

CONTENTS

FOREWORD

It takes two and a half seconds to drop from the top of monstrous Southern Ocean waves. Your stomach is left over your head while your body tenses, anticipating the impact of solid water. But the nervousness gives way to the indescribable thrill of surging forward at 30 knots. This is the essence of the Whitbread Round the World Race.

Sure, there are doldrums and storms, friendly ports and potential glory. But if I were to sum up the Whitbread in one word, it would be *speed*. Over its 25-year history, the Whitbread has evolved from an adventurous voyage (race) to as intense a competition as any in sailing. To participate in this race, a crew member must have impeccable credentials, a highly motivated attitude, resourcefulness, and the ability to endure hardship and discomfort for weeks at a time.

In the past, just finishing the Whitbread was a major accomplishment, but not anymore. With the glare of on-board television cameras broadcasting to satellites and continuous updates on the Internet, millions (probably billions) of people followed the 1997–98 Whitbread Race. Finishing is impressive, but winning is the paramount goal.

Over the 31,600-mile, nine-leg course, anything could happen and often did. All nine teams treated every mile like a day race. Even so, there were elements of conservatism in the back of every watch captain's mind. In a track meet, runners will sprint the final distance as the finish line nears. But in this Whitbread Race, the sprinting began as the fleet crossed the starting line, and the winner never stopped sprinting.

George Collins, *Chessie Racing*'s founder and skipper, and Kathy Alexander, *Chessie Racing*'s press officer, capture the essence of the Whitbread through the eyes and ears of *Chessie Racing*. They traveled to every port, and George sailed on three of the legs. They started observing and recording this emotional roller-coaster ride from Day 1 and present it here for all of us on shore to enjoy.

Gary Jobson
ESPN Sailing Commentator

PREFACE

During the Whitbread Round the World Race and my time with *Chessie Racing* (nicknamed *Chessie* by both crew and fans), I was overwhelmed by the interest in *Chessie Racing* and the Whitbread, but I was amazed that even after the race people stopped me on the street with questions. As a result I talked to George Collins about writing a book about the experience, so the fans could get a behind-the-scenes view of life with *Chessie Racing*. After all, we had the contacts, my "quotes file" (which I used for press releases), and more than 10,000 photographs documenting the story. A few additional interviews, and we were ready to go.

Through *Chessie Racing: The Story of Maryland's Entry in the 1997–1998 Whitbread Round the World Race,* we hope to show the hard work, determination, expertise, and continual learning required; the fun and excitement enjoyed; and the respect and caring involved. The entire *Chessie* crew willingly worked long hours in less than ideal settings. They used their expertise, discovered new places and different cultures, and reveled in the excitement. But perhaps what was most enlightening was their respect and concern for the world around them.

The Whitbreaders marveled at the wildlife and were saddened by the pollution they saw. They would not throw their trash overboard; they stored it and disposed of it at port, where the shore crews recycled their trash. Everyone took time to talk to the people, sometimes struggling over language barriers, and learn about the local customs and beliefs. The *Chessie* crew, in particular, visited schools around the world and e-mailed students following the race, sharing their experiences and knowledge.

Unless otherwise stated, the quotes used in this book are from personal conversations, my "quote file," or the Whitbread website (www.whitbread.org) produced by Quokka Sports.

Kathy Alexander

CHESSIE RACING

Chessie Comes to Life

Chessie: sea monster or folklore, fact or fantasy? Story has it that Chessie, first sighted in the early 1800s, lives in the Chesapeake Bay. Is she a relative of the legendary Loch Ness monster? Or can she be explained away as a giant anaconda, a giant squid, or a manatee? Despite numerous sightings, some as recent as the 1990s, the legend remains shrouded in mystery. However, in 1997 Chessie was brought to life, by a man of Scottish ancestry, in the form of a Whitbread 60 (W60), a sleek, high-tech racing yacht. This latter-day Chessie became the "kids' boat," one of the most loved syndicates in the 1997–98 Whitbread Round the World fleet.

The Whitbread Round the World Race, commonly referred to simply as the Whitbread, began 25 years ago as a Corinthian test of endurance. Over the years, it has obtained the highest global profile in the international sailing calendar and has become universally acknowledged as the world's premier ocean race. Every four years, a new fleet of racing yachts circumnavigates the globe, following the route of the old clipper

Chessie Racing represented the United States and the Chesapeake Bay Region in the 1997–98 Whitbread Round the World Race.

ships around the tip of Africa (Cape of Good Hope), across the southern Indian and Pacific Oceans, around the tip of South America (Cape Horn), and back to England. For nine months and 31,600 miles, the world's top professional sailors compete in this sailing marathon, pushing themselves and their yachts to the limit and beyond.

In the late 1960s, the London Sunday *Times* sponsored the Golden Globe Race. Eight boats set out, but numerous problems and accidents forced most of the competitors to withdraw. Eventually, one boat managed to complete the course. Surprisingly, from that dubious attempt, the adventure of the endeavor caught the imagination of the Royal Naval Sailing Association (RNSA), which wanted to use the race as a training vehicle for its cadets. Over a pint of Whitbread beer, Admiral Otto Steiner of the RNSA convinced Colonel Bill Whitbread of the Whitbread Brewery to sponsor another race,

the Whitbread Round the World Race. With proper organization and preparation, they believed it could be done relatively safely. In September 1973, the first Whitbread Round the World Race sailed from England, the home of the Whitbread Brewery, and successfully circumnavigated the globe.

The first fleet consisted of sturdy cruising yachts manned by adventurers and a few serious yachtsmen. Despite many accidents and three deaths, the race grew, becoming increasingly competitive. The cruisers and adventurers were soon left behind and replaced by high-tech racing machines crewed by top-notch professional sailors.

This well-known and highly respected global race first came to the United States during its 1993–94 competition. Gary Jobson, ESPN's sailing commentator, and Mark Fischer, chief executive officer (CEO) of Blakeslee Group, lobbied the Whitbread Round the World Race Committee to make a combination of Baltimore and Annapolis the U.S. stopover port for the 1993–94 race. Fort Lauderdale, Florida, won the bid. The Race Committee believed that an ocean race should take place on an ocean, not a bay, but Baltimore and Annapolis made a good impression and laid the groundwork.

In 1995, the Race Committee, wanting greater visibility in and participation from the United States, returned to the idea of a combination of Baltimore and Annapolis as a potential stopover venue for the 1997–98 race. Again, Gary Jobson and Mark Fischer spearheaded the effort. To convince the Race Committee that the business community would support their efforts, they enlisted the help of amateur sailor George Collins, president and CEO of the Baltimore-based mutual fund company, T. Rowe Price Associates, Inc. Visiting the area, the Race Committee met city and state officials, toured Baltimore and Annapolis, and took a helicopter ride over the proposed race course. Eventually, the entourage convened in one of T. Rowe Price's conference rooms overlooking Baltimore's dazzling Inner Harbor.

As George remembers it, "The day was perfect—sun shining with a strong, steady breeze out of the west. Nothing would deny us our dream. Even when asked, 'Is the weather always like this?' we carefully answered, 'Sometimes even better.' The meeting went smoothly enough, but it became apparent our dream hinged on having a local entry. I scribbled, 'Can we do this?' on a paper napkin and handed it to Mark. He took the question in a broad sense and nodded his assurance. After much pitching and no commitment from the race chairman, I popped the question, 'Are you telling me that having an entry from Baltimore is a make-or-break deciding factor?' The chairman said yes. I paused and offered, 'I don't see why we can't have a boat.' And Baltimore became a stop-

over." Afterward, Mark called George and asked whether he knew what he had said. "Sure, I don't see why we can't have a boat in the race," reiterated George.

That meeting set everything in motion—organizing the management team for the syndicate; researching boat designs, race and crew requirements including housing, logistics, nutrition, and training; seeking sponsorship; and reviewing résumés for the crew. And that was just at the syndicate level. Similar maneuverings were going full-tilt at the port level, as well. Gary Jobson, sought after by both the syndicate and the port, decided that he should play an advisory role for each. The weight of the project fell on the shoulders of the note passers, George Collins and Mark Fischer. They got to work immediately, recruiting Jim Allsopp, director of sales and marketing for North Sails of North America, to round out the management committee.

With the 1997–98 race, the complexion of

George J. Collins, founder and skipper of *Chessie Racing:* "I grew up in a hard-driving middle-class family, playing blue-collar sports—baseball, basketball, and football—in school. I didn't learn to sail until after high school."

4

Jim Allsopp, member of the management committee and coskipper of Leg 1, has participated in the design and construction of sails for racing boats and premier offshore cruising yachts and has managed sail development programs for America's Cup and Whitbread campaigns. He was the 1979 world champion in Star boats. (Photograph by Miguel Wilkens)

the Whitbread would change. Not a race of multiple boat designs sailing around the globe, it would be a one-design race of W60s. Designed specifically for the race, the W60 had been introduced in 1993–94. Previously, maxis (70+ feet, two-masted racing yachts carrying a crew of 16 or more) had been considered the fastest and most seaworthy vessels for this race. Smaller, lighter, and less expensive, the W60 speed was never doubted; sturdiness and durability were the concerns. Pitted against the heavier and more expensive maxis, the W60s proved themselves up to the task. In fact, their impressive performance persuaded the Race Committee to make future Whitbreads one-class races. The 1997–98 Whitbread would be the first one-design race of W60s.

The management team's first act was to visit Bruce Farr's office in Annapolis. "Make us a fast boat," George told Farr and his design team. Bruce Farr, considered the world's foremost designer of racing sailboats, had immigrated from New Zealand and now made Annapolis his home. Soft-spoken and unassuming, he was known for pushing the frontiers of yacht design. With winning

yachts in the ¼-ton, ½-ton, ¾-ton, 1-ton, and IMS (International Measurement System) championships to his credit, Bruce eventually found himself designing 8 of the 10 W60s that would start the 1997–98 Whitbread Round the World Race. His odds of having a winner in the race were extremely good.

Designing competing boats, Bruce developed a system to protect each syndicate's input and design. "Often I am in this situation. There is a lot of research that goes into designing a boat like this. I categorize the research into levels—each successive level offering more research and a better possibility of a winning boat. The competitors decide how much research they can and are willing to buy. Then I meet with the crew and get their input on the boat and weather expectations. Ultimately each boat's design is based on a combination of the research level purchased, its crew's input, and the anticipated weather and sea conditions. The competitors know my system and are comfortable with it."

Weather, routing, and expected sea conditions were analyzed before the boat was designed. Were the Whitbread a round-the-buoy race, it would have simplified matters immensely. But the Whitbread circumnavigates the globe. It crosses the Doldrums (the area of calms north of the equator), known for its virtual lack of wind and extreme heat, which can cause hull and sail delamination; it crosses the Southern Ocean (mariners' name for the southern Pacific and Indian Oceans), known for its icebergs, 40-foot, bone-crushing waves, and sustained winds of 50+ knots. In defining the optimum courses, sailing angles, and forces acting on the boat, Farr's design team uses a computer to help analyze research data. With the analysis in hand, they develop the desired hull, keel, and sail plan.

DIMENSIONS OF THE "TYPICAL" W60*

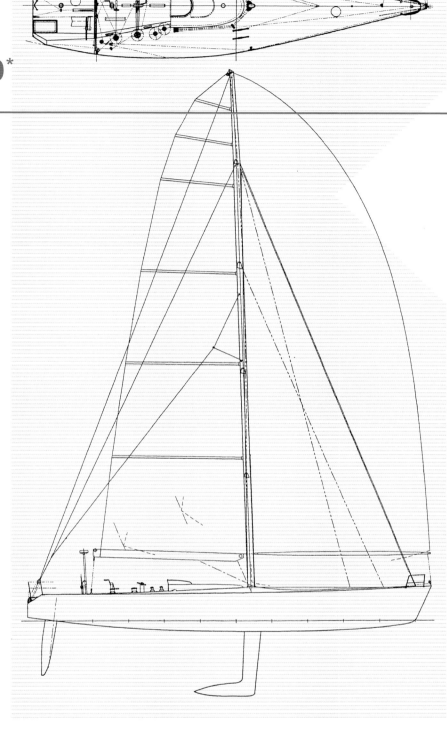

Length overall	64 ft
Beam	17.2 ft
Draft	12.3 ft
Weight	29,700 lb
Mainsail area	1,259.4 sq ft
Jib area	893.4 sq ft
Spinnaker area (maximum)	3,229.2 sq ft
Mast height	85 ft
Keel bulb	7 tons
Number of crew	11–12

*Called a *box rule,* the W60 Rule was developed to ensure that the boats performed similarly. It set a series of technical specifications, usually maximum limits; the boat had to fit within those limits. These restrictions, however, still left a little room for adjustments that each boat could take advantage of, possibly giving it the edge needed to win.

The difference between a W60 and most yachts is the use of the water ballast system, tanks on each side of the yacht that can pump as much as two and a half tons of water in and out as needed for added ballast.

Using a velocity prediction program (VPP), they can design and virtually race the boat in all conditions, determine its stability, find out what works and what does not, make adjustments, and even predict the boat's performance under a variety of scenarios.

Farr predicted a better and faster breed of W60s for this race, since many of the 1993–94 Whitbread limitations had been removed. "This time, a masthead spinnaker [a large, billowing headsail that attaches to the top of the mast and is used for sailing downwind] would be permitted on all legs, and the maximum weight for these sails would be removed, making the rigs much more powerful in strong winds." In addition, significant changes in design, not apparent to the untrained eye, would increase speed and stability. As Farr explained, "The boats had their longitudinal center of buoyancy farther forward, were deeper and more veed in the bow, and were generally fuller around the mast

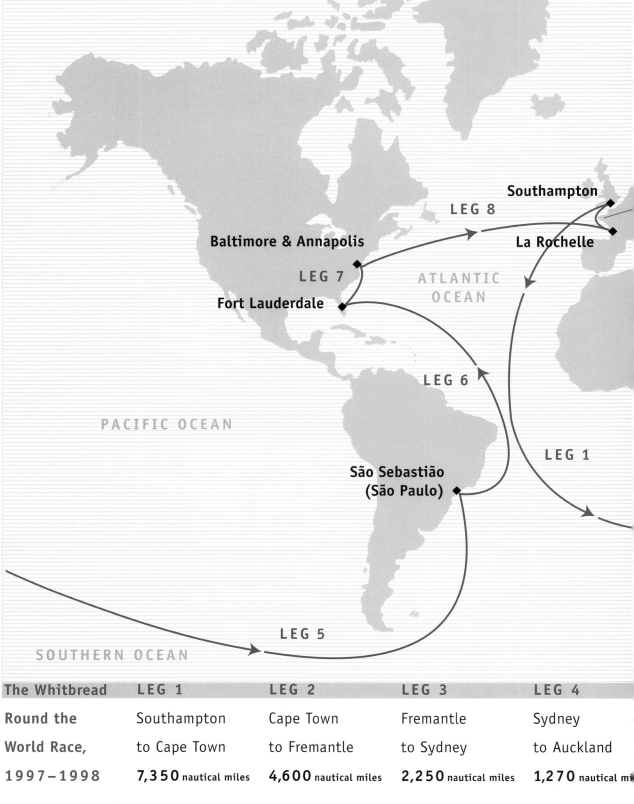

The Whitbread	LEG 1	LEG 2	LEG 3	LEG 4
Round the	Southampton	Cape Town	Fremantle	Sydney
World Race,	to Cape Town	to Fremantle	to Sydney	to Auckland
1997–1998	**7,350** nautical miles	**4,600** nautical miles	**2,250** nautical miles	**1,270** nautical mi*

area. The average boat was a little narrower and had smaller keel fins and deeper rudders."

For the boats to reach and maintain maximum speeds, they needed increased sail area and stability. W60s obtain the stability to compensate for the increased sail area by using a water ballast system. Up to two and a half tons of seawater can be pumped into and out of tanks on either side of the boat, thereby increasing the weight holding the

boat upright against the heeling effect of the sails. Two and a half tons of water in the tank, while sailing upwind, is roughly equivalent to 28 crew members hiking hard on the rail (sitting on the high side of the boat to add weight). *Chessie*'s ballast system, run by a Johnson impeller pump, consisted of four tanks on each side of the boat. Assisted by gravity, these tanks could be filled or transferred in four to five minutes or dumped in a minute and a half.

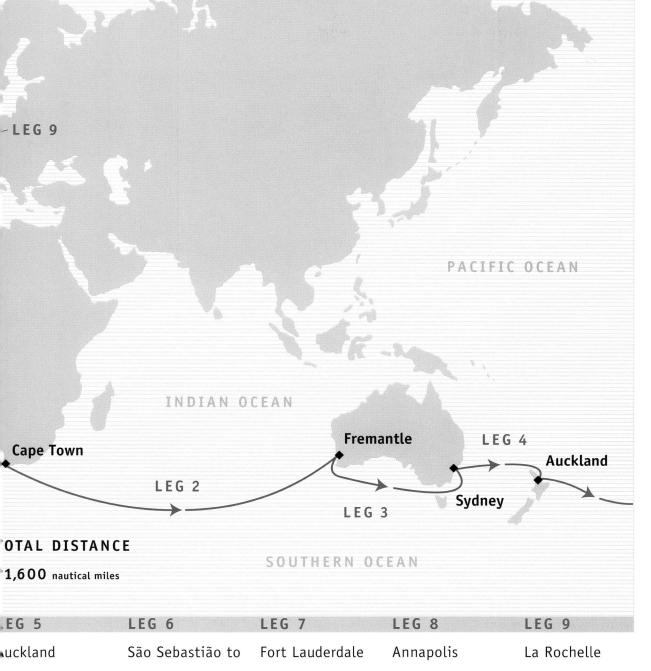

LEG 9

PACIFIC OCEAN

INDIAN OCEAN

Fremantle

LEG 4

Auckland

Cape Town

LEG 2

Sydney

LEG 3

OTAL DISTANCE

1,600 nautical miles

SOUTHERN OCEAN

LEG 5	LEG 6	LEG 7	LEG 8	LEG 9
uckland	São Sebastião to	Fort Lauderdale	Annapolis	La Rochelle
o São Sebastião	Fort Lauderdale	to Baltimore	to La Rochelle	to Southampton
,670 nautical miles	4,750 nautical miles	870 nautical miles	3,390 nautical miles	450 nautical miles

The next design step was to determine the sail plan configuration and rig. Although fewer sails were allowed in the 1997–98 Whitbread, new sail shapes and materials promised to improve downwind and close-reaching performance. (A close reach is when the wind is within a few points forward of the beam, or middle of the boat.) Boats were limited to 17 sails per leg and only 38 sails for the entire race, including replacements. Again, weather, routing, and expected sea conditions were considered in developing sails, determining when they would be used, and estimating how long they would last. Because the boats were so similar in design, sail development was critical to the race results and continued throughout the race. By the start in Southampton, England, *Chessie* had developed only 20 of her allotted 38 sails for the race. The management team used lessons learned on the first few legs when developing the remaining sails. *Chessie*

Dave Scott was born in
Canterbury, England, and
moved to the United
States when he was 12
years old. He was on
sailing teams in high
school and college and
then joined North Sails,
where he is in charge of
designing, testing, and
writing tuning guides
for the newest, cutting-
edge race boats.

planned to monitor the sails' "onboard lifetime," ordering replacement sails in time to
be delivered at the next stopover. "We left 6
of the total permitted 38-sail inventory open,
in case of crew error," explained Dave Scott,
Chessie's watch captain and sailmaker.

Chessie had two options for the keel shape.
The management team mulled over the
L-shaped or T-shaped keel. Each seemed to
have advantages and disadvantages. With
the competition so intense and no one knowing how much research the other syndicates
had purchased, the syndicates, *Chessie*
included, kept their keel shapes closely
guarded secrets.

The W60s were built for speed, not com-
fort. Since weight slows a boat, everything
used to build the boat, as well as everything
carried on it, had to be weighed. Some equipment was mandated, and other items were
deemed worth carrying despite their weight.
Below deck was a cramped, Spartan world,

loaded with high-tech communication equipment, a desalinator to make fresh water from
seawater, and two engines—a main engine,
for maneuvering in port but not permitted
for use during racing except in an emergency,
and a donkey engine (the workhorse),
which ran the ballast pump, desalinator, and
battery recharger. Personal amenities consisted merely of six pipe berths along each
side (nylon mesh framed by aluminum
tubing and weighing 3 kg each); a minimal
galley (two burners and a sink—8 kg including the cabinetry and fuel); a toilet (minus a
toilet seat); and six hooks on each side for
foul weather gear. The minimal storage space
allowed each crew member only a gear bag
(about the size of a two-gallon plastic bag)
in which to store personal effects, including
extra clothing. The cabin floor and pipe
berths doubled as storage for sails and the
freeze-dried food needed for each particular
leg.

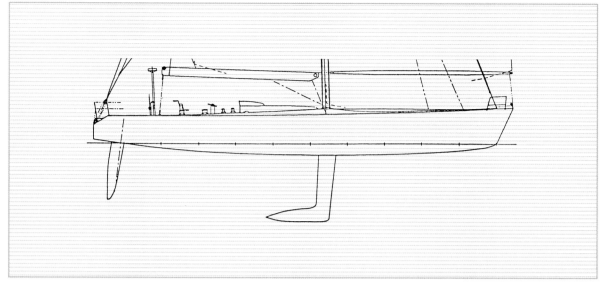

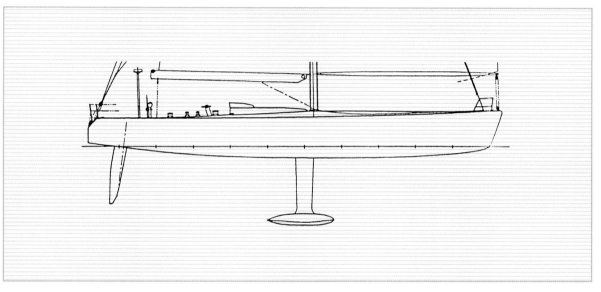

"The L looked better in highly loaded conditions upwind. The T looked to have less drag downwind and in light air," explained Farr. "But early testing showed no clear-cut winner."

The boatbuilders shaved weight wherever possible, but the race rules specified a minimum weight for the boat and its equipment. Heaters were permitted. Originally, *Chessie* tried a small heater to help dry foul weather gear but scrapped it because it could not do the job. Deemed definitely worth the weight were the masthead heavy-air sails. Although they decrease stability, their larger total sail area dramatically increases speed. To compensate, designers added each pound saved on nonessentials to the keel bulb for more stability. Farr stressed that, "while our concerns focus on the right shape, good engineering, and designing the fastest and most comfortable boat we can provide, it cannot and will not be done at the cost of stability."

The communications equipment, a required and necessary use of weight, consisted of a single-side band radio and four computers—two SATCOM Cs for weather and tactical/navigational information, one dedicated

Two crew members, on different watch duties, shared a hook for foul weather gear. Painting the boat's interior was considered an unnecessary luxury and unnecessary weight.

SATCOM B for communication with the Race Committee, and one SATCOM B for video and still-photo transfer. Alone in the middle of the ocean, this equipment provided the crews' only link to civilization and allowed the Race Committee to track the boat. The video package included digital cameras with remote receptacles, a full editing desk with waterproof computer, and a full SATCOM B system to upload assembled images to the race office. A microwave uplink

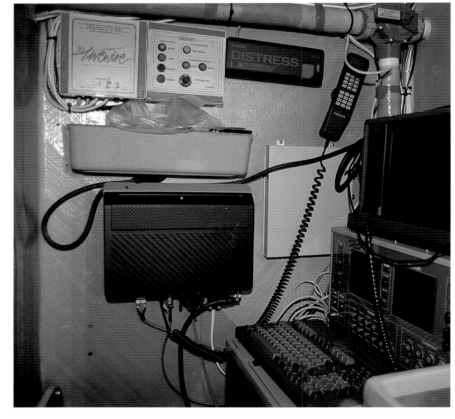

Top: The satellite dish required special insulation on the forward bulkhead to shield the crew from microwaves. *Bottom:* Video equipment.

system enabled the crew to send live video. Each boat had an Inmarsat B SATCOM, a satellite antenna located in the bow. If all of this equipment failed, a 406 mHz satellite EPIRB (emergency position-indicating radio beacon) could send distress signals. Also, each sailor always carried a personal EPIRB, with an installed radio direction finder to locate a man-overboard quickly. Finally, *Chessie*'s electrical system powered the water pump, bilge pump, a few house lights, the running lights, and the trimming lights. According to the race rules, a boat's running lights must be displayed from dusk to dawn.

The crews of the W60s willingly made numerous sacrifices for the ultimate thrill ride. These boats could sustain speeds in excess of 30 knots, which more than compensated for the miserable living conditions. Halfway through the journey, Grant "Fuzz" Spanhake, *Chessie*'s watch captain, quipped that "the Human Rights Commission should check into our living conditions. Animals have it better." Missing were heaters, air conditioners, showers, tables and chairs, entertainment centers, and basically anything landlubbers consider essential.

During the design process, numerous other tasks needed prompt attention: sponsorship, a name and logo, and eventually the construction of the boat. Financing a Whitbread syndicate usually costs between $10 million and $16 million. The original plan had George Collins donating seed money to build the boat, with the bulk of the financing coming from corporate sponsors. Some things never go according to plan, and *Chessie Racing*'s sponsorship fell into that category.

George, who is on the board of directors of the Living Classrooms Foundation (a Baltimore-based nonprofit educational organization that uses sailing as a vehicle to build self-esteem and job skills for at-risk students),

Grant Spanhake, better known as "Fuzz," is a New Zealand native who learned to sail at an early age. A two-time Whitbread veteran, Fuzz moved to Annapolis, Maryland, where he consults with Farr Associates and North Sails.

approached Parker Rockefeller, senior vice president of the Living Classrooms Foundation, about his entry in the race. George proposed partnering *Chessie Racing* and the Living Classrooms Foundation to bring the magic of the Whitbread Round the World Race to students and classrooms all over the world. Parker jumped at the opportunity. George agreed to donate $2.5 million to the foundation to build the boat, additional monies for sails, and the necessary funds to develop a nine-month curriculum teaching math, science, history, and other academic subjects based on the journey of the new flagship, *Chessie Racing*. Parker would have to secure funds to run the program. The Whitbread Education Project was born.

Partnering with a nonprofit organization provided an avenue for individuals, as well as corporations, to become sponsors. It also diluted some of the event's commercialism

Parker Rockefeller, senior vice president of the Living Classrooms Foundation (*left*), got some sailing tips from John Kostecki (*right*).

and gave the crew an additional reason to win—for the students. With the Living Classrooms becoming an integral part of the *Chessie Racing* team, Parker Rockefeller became a member of the management committee. Although everyone accepted it willingly, there was a negative side to the partnership. It restricted which corporations could be approached for sponsorship. George would not have *Chessie* sporting alcohol or tobacco logos. "This boat is an education tool, and we won't be sending kids unhealthy messages," he said.

While Parker sought financing for the Whitbread Education Project, securing suitable sponsorship for the syndicate itself fell to Mark Fischer and Kathy Alexander. Although their options were limited, their determination was not. They made a list of domestic companies with a global consumer base that used sports to market their products; however, their efforts were often frustrated by

Top: **Kathy Alexander,**
***Chessie*'s marketing**
specialist and public
relations officer, dealt
with the press, the
sponsors, the volun-
teers, the fans, and the
students. *Bottom:* **Mark**
Fischer, president of
***Chessie*'s management**
committee, coskippered
Legs 1 and 2. His wife,
Stephanie, was a mem-
ber of the shore crew,
drew the design for the
***Chessie* logo, and ar-**
ranged the crew's
accommodations around
the world.

replies such as "We only sponsor 'real' sports." Interestingly, although U.S. companies did not consider sailing a "real" sport, those in the rest of the world did. In fact, soccer and sailing are two of the most popular sports in the global community, while baseball and football are, for the most part, limited to the U.S. audience. Making matters worse, sailing had not been considered a spectator sport—until the 1997–98 Whitbread Round the World Race. Quokka Sports had agreed to develop a website (www.whitbread. org) to follow the race, which became one of the most popular websites on the Internet during the race.

Often, Mark and Kathy found themselves educating potential sponsors about sailing and the Whitbread Race before even mentioning *Chessie.* Although a daunting job, with help from volunteer Jim Patton, Mark and Kathy did enlist supplier sponsors, including Douglas Gill (performance clothing),

Revo Sunglasses, Open Air Wear (fleece wear), Johnson Pumps (marine pumps), and Zodiac of North America (inflatable boats). By race time, however, the syndicate had failed to secure financial corporate sponsorship. Would the entire effort go for naught? No, George had promised a local boat, and he would not go back on his word. The supplier sponsors reaped the rewards of their association with *Chessie.* Based on media analysis, she reached an audience exceeding 24 million people and earned goodwill around the globe.

When it came to naming the boat, George looked to his wife, Maureen. "If she is representing the Chesapeake, why not name her *Chessie* for the Chesapeake's legendary sea monster?" she suggested. Add the word *racing* to emphasize the purpose, and the syndicate had a name—*Chessie Racing.*

Now *Chessie Racing* needed a logo. A playful, friendly logo seemed appropriate, consid-

Above: Bill Koppler (lead boatbuilder—*left*), Eric Goetz (*center*), and Bryan Fishback (*right*) examine their work.
Right: Flipping *Chessie*'s hull

CHESSIE RACING'S SUPPLIER SPONSORS

Annapolis Quarterly

Baltimore Marine Center

Chesapeake Bay Spyce

Classic Catering People

Communications
 Electronics, Inc.

DIGEX

Douglas Gill

Graul's Market, Inc.

Hale Intermodal

Johnson Pump

Jos. A. Banks Clothiers

Linganore Winecellars

Maryland Nautical
 Sales, Inc.

Maryland Screenprinters

McGarvey's Restaurant

Mercury Marine

NASA

Open Air Wear

Reese Press

Revo Sunglasses

Rusty Scupper
 Restaurant

Southwest Spirit/
 RGE, Inc.

Suunto

Team McLube

Yale Cordage/Aramid
 Rigging

Zodiac of North America

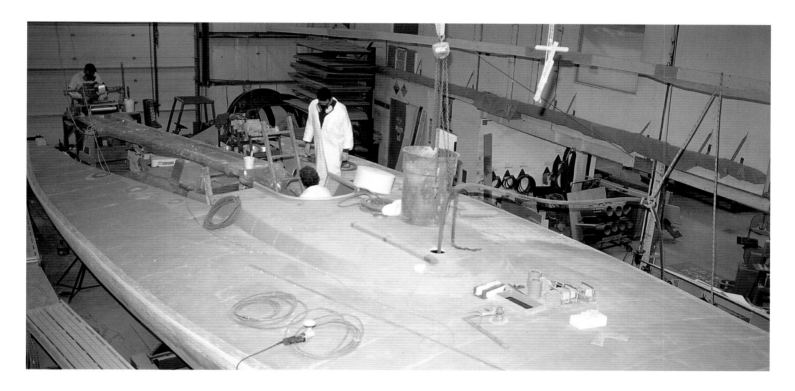

ering the Living Classrooms connection. Again, Maureen had the answer—a friendly sea monster. Done. Stephanie Fischer, Mark's wife, whipped up a rough sketch of just such a character, wrapping it around the globe and putting Revo sunglasses on it. With a little touch-up and some added color from the graphic artists at The Blakeslee Group, *Chessie* had a very kid-friendly logo.

The management committee believed that having the best possible boat was imperative to being competitive in the Whitbread. As George said, "No boat can win a race for you, but a boat can lose a race for even the best sailors." With the basic design agreed upon, the next critical step was securing a construction manager. Bryan Fishback's name was mentioned. Considered one of the best in his field, Bryan had worked with Farr in the past and had an engineering degree in naval architecture from State University of New York Maritime College; he was hired. "*Chessie*

scored a major coup in persuading Bryan to join the *Chessie* team," claimed Farr.

Bryan was a newlywed, and *Chessie* got a bonus—his wife, Kerry. Also a sailing enthusiast, Kerry was hired as *Chessie*'s liaison and traveling correspondent to the Living Classrooms Foundation. She also helped manage the Whitbread Education Project.

Because it was an American syndicate, George insisted that *Chessie* be built in America. Eric Goetz Custom Boats was a natural. Located in Bristol, Rhode Island, the company had begun constructing cold-molded wood boats in 1975 and had grown with the transition in boat building technology.

Eric Goetz, founder and owner of the company that bears his name, received his B.A. in anthropology from Brown University and attended the Rhode Island School of Design and the Hall Institute. He has put together an extensive résumé, from sailing to

Top: Because of hazard-
ous dust and fumes,
the boatbuilders wore
protective masks.
Right: Installing the
ballast system.

In measuring the keel against the plumb line, absolute precision was required.

boat building. Some of the boats he built include *America 3, Stars & Stripes,* and *The Card* (maxi designed by Bruce Farr—1989–90 Whitbread). Now Goetz was commissioned to build two of the new W60s (*America's Challenge,* designed by Alan Andrews, and *Chessie*).

Quite enthusiastic about his latest high-tech projects, Eric explained, "These kinds of boats really benefit from our building techniques. Where strength over the long haul is as important as light weight and stiffness, our construction, using prepreg Kevlar [the same material used in bulletproof vests] over foam and balsa core, really makes a difference. We know our boats will give their crews every possible technical advantage in the Whitbread."

Marrying old traditions and state-of-the-art science, a team of 15 boat-building artists employed ideas and skills dating back to the early days of shipbuilding along with technologies used to build space shuttles. Each component had to be precise to ensure the sturdiness needed; there was no margin for error. Sections were designed and redesigned until absolute perfection was achieved.

The deck and hull were created in two pieces. Before the actual construction began, full-sized molds of the hull and the deck were built out of wood frames and planks; the molds held the shape of the hull and deck until they were compressed and baked in the oven. The hull and deck were built using a sandwichlike construction technique in which a polyvinyl chloride (PVC) foam core is sandwiched between two skins of Kevlar fabric impregnated with epoxy resin. Using technology learned from jet fighter builders, the boatbuilders sealed each piece in a gigantic plastic bag, connected it to a very powerful vacuum pump to compress the Kevlar

Applying the final coat
of paint

fibers, epoxy resin, and foam core into one solid piece, and then placed it in an oven the size of a house to bake overnight at 90°C (194°F). The final result was the outer skin for the hull and the deck, tough enough to resist the tremendous forces of the Southern Ocean when surfing at more than 30 knots.

Upon completion of the deck and hull, a special team of boatbuilders carefully bolted winches and deck gear to the deck and lowered the main and auxiliary engines inside the hull. Finally, the boatbuilders joined the deck and hull, allowing the engine mechanic, electrician, plumber, rigger, and painters to get to work.

During the next five weeks, many tasks had to be completed before *Chessie* could make her maiden voyage to her home waters, the Chesapeake Bay. The mast and keel arrived from New Zealand, and the lead bulb came from Mexico. The mast, 85 feet high,

was made of aluminum and weighed a ton, about the weight of a small car. The lead bulb, attached to the bottom of the keel, provided the boat's stability. It weighed about seven tons, or approximately half the weight of the entire boat.

Throughout the entire building process, everything was weighed, from the bulkheads to the glue used to attach them. Even the paint dust was swept up and weighed. Why? Every ounce saved could be converted to more lead in the bulb for added stability. "I'm happy to report that *Chessie* is a very trim monster and passed her weigh-in with ease," smiled Bryan.

After more than twenty thousand man-hours, the proud crew lowered *Chessie* into the water at Little Harbor Marina in Portsmouth, Rhode Island. "She's so sophisticated and high-tech, yet built by hand, a real work of art," said Jon Holstrom, one of *Chessie*'s 15 boatbuilders.

Chessie was finally
lowered into the water.

Chessie's Crew Takes Shape

As word got out that a Baltimore/Annapolis group was building a Whitbread syndicate, résumés started arriving. *Chessie* received over three hundred résumés from around the world. Most were from competent and talented regatta sailors, some were from adventurers, and some were from professional offshore racers. The management committee pored over the résumés, narrowing the field. They determined early on that *Chessie* would have an all-male crew. Although the management committee respected the abilities of female sailors, the combination of cramped quarters and length of the legs made a coed crew impractical. All of the syndicates seemed to come to the same conclusion.

Usually, the first step in selecting a crew is naming a skipper. *Chessie* announced its intentions late for a Whitbread syndicate; most of the big-name skippers had already signed with other syndicates. Others would not be available for nine months straight or did not believe that *Chessie* would get to the starting gate. Management decided that rotating some of America's well-respected, highly accomplished sailors would be the next best option. Gavin Brady, John Kostecki, Ken Read, Tony Rey, Dee Smith, and Mike Toppa were contacted.

The crew would require

- **a navigator,** who determines where the boat is and where it should be going; monitors weather systems, currents, and all boat systems, including batteries and the water maker; and advises the skipper on the desired course

- **two watch captains,** who are second in command to the skipper, each running the boat during his watch, with one on duty at all times; a watch captain determines which sails should be used, manages boat speed and crew, and positions the boat in consultation with the navigator and the tactician or skipper

- **a crew boss,** who supervises everyone except the afterguard (namely, skipper, navigator, and watch captains)

- **a tactician,** who determines and calls tactics (i.e., monitors current and wind, determines where the boat is positioned vis-à-vis other boats, and advises the skipper and navigator on course restrictions and strategy); if not listed, performed by the skipper

- **helmsmen/drivers,** who steer the boat

- **bowmen,** who work the front of the boat, changing sails and climbing the mast during sail changes, if necessary

- **trimmers,** who trim the sails to adjust to wind direction, improving speed

- **grinders,** who trim the sails, using the pedestal grinder or winches, and hoist crew members up the mast when needed

- **sailmakers,** who design, develop, and repair sails

- **medics** (onboard emergency medical tacticians)

- **cameramen** (onboard photographers and video cameramen)

- **boatbuilders,** who repair structural damage while at sea

- **boat maintenance workers,** who repair mechanical damage while at sea

- **rigger,** who repairs rigging while at sea

- **cook,** who prepares meals by adding water to freeze-dried food and cleans up (a duty taken by crew members on a rotating schedule)

With limited crew space, crew members would need to serve in multiple capacities.

Phone calls, faxes, interviews, and trials—the applicants vying for the 12 sought-after positions came and went. Most of the sailors capable of competing in the Whitbread have sailed with or against each other numerous times; at the very least, they know each other by reputation. As the referral calls were made, the potential crew list was refined. Their sailing résumés boasted premier ocean races, including prior Whitbreads, America's Cups, Admirals' Cups, World Championships, and the Olympics, as well as the management of boat programs.

Now the crew needed a training vessel. Without corporate funding, *Chessie* did not have the funds to purchase a used W60. The

Rick Deppe (bowman/ mechanic/cameraman), an Annapolitan transplant originally from England, was one of *Chessie*'s first crew members. With his dry sense of humor and keen knowledge of the boat, Rick became a valuable member of the team. He also performed numerous acrobatic feats at the top of the mast, providing *Chessie*'s medics with lots of practice on live subjects.

**Jerry Kirby (*left*) and
Greg Gendell (*right*)
worked the bow.**

next best option was a Corel 45, a very competitive class of boat capable of accommodating a 12-man crew. George Collins had one built. It served as *Chessie*'s training boat, testing the sailing ability of crew candidates and their ability to work as a team. At sea for long stretches, teamwork is vital. According to Rick Deppe, George's boat manager and crew for his string of raceboats, "What would make a good crew was its ability to work together in all situations." Eventually, the sailing crew began to take shape. In addition to regattas, practice runs, and deliveries, the Corel competed at the Southern Ocean Racing Conference (SORC) regatta held every winter, was first to finish in the Fort Lauderdale–Key West Race in International Measurement System (IMS) championships, won the Miami to Montego Race, placed third in the Annapolis to Newport Race, and did Leg 7 of the Whitbread a year before the actual

race leg. Although the Corel allowed the crew to sail together as a team, it did not familiarize them with a W60 and its capabilities. When *Chessie Racing* was launched, the crew started training fast and hard on it, sailing up and down the Eastern Seaboard and across the Atlantic Ocean.

The support crew also began to take shape. Rob Slade, who had worked with the Baltimore County and Howard County Fire Departments, the Maryland Police Corps, and the Maryland State Police Training Academy developing, implementing, and monitoring specialized classes and who was the strength and conditioning coach for the University of Maryland Baltimore County, contacted *Chessie*. He had heard about the syndicate and wanted to be a part of it, not as a sailor but as its strength coach. A sailor in his own right, Rob knew that the Whitbread required a rare combination of strength, speed, agility, balance, and endurance. He

Stu Wilson (*left*) and
Dave Scott (*right*)
studied the sails care-
fully while trimming.

Jerry Kirby adjusted the
rigging at the first
spreader.

Rob Slade (*left*) was chosen by his colleagues as the 1998 National Strength and Conditioning Association (NSCA) Big South Conference Strength and Conditioning College Professional of the Year. Rudi Rodriguez (*right*), "Dr. Rudi," traveled to every port and soon became known as "the Whitbread doctor." When the crews and their families had an ailment or a concern, they asked Dr. Rudi to check it out.

understood that certain muscle groups would be worked more than others and that speed in short bursts, similar to a sprinter's speed, would be needed. Rob also knew that sailors' schedules seldom put them in the same place at the same time, which further complicated his task. Bringing exercises from various sports, Rob developed the ideal workout program—mobile, flexible, thorough—specifically for the *Chessie* crew. And it could be done alone or as a team.

The sailing crew worked out in the gym constantly. No matter where they traveled, alone or as a team, Rob secured the use of a nearby gym. Each crew member had to forward his results to Rob on a monthly basis for consistent monitoring, and Rob met the team at regattas to test the crew's progress.

Rob worked in unison with *Chessie's* newly hired team physician, Rudi Rodriguez, also a sailor. An emergency sports physician who had worked with the Italian and Australian America's Cup teams in San Diego, Dr. Rudi also wanted to contribute to the home-team effort. He got right to work, organizing a team of local physicians, with a broad range of specialties, to volunteer their time examining the crew and determining who was physically up to the journey.

According to race rules, each member of the crew had to pass a medical examination "not more than six months before the start." The results required approval by the Whitbread Committee's medical adviser. The

PHYSICIANS AND TRAINERS

Rudi Rodriguez, M.D.

Pen Alexander, M.D.

Hugh Baugher, M.D.

Captain Dale Crutchley (paramedic/fire captain)

Stephen Faust, M.D.

Joseph Fiore, D.C., F.A.C.C.O.

Robert Greenfield, M.D.

Stephen Hiltabilde, M.D.

Ed Holt, M.D.

David Johnson, D.D.S.

Peggy Jones, R.N., C.E.N., C.R.T.

Roxanne Moore (nutritionist)

Maria Scott, M.D.

Rob Slade, S.C.S.

Douglas Wallop, P.T.

Juan Vila (*right*),
navigator, gave George a
tour of the nav station.
Juan is from Spain, and
this would be his third
Whitbread as navigator.

Chessie crew passed easily. In fact, *Chessie* had
the most physically fit crew in the fleet.

Chessie augmented the crew's knowledge
with specific courses. Rick took a Yanmar
diesel course, which helped him repair mechanical breakdowns while at sea. Juan Vila
(*Chessie*'s navigator), George Collins, Mark
Fischer, Fuzz Spanhake, and Dave Scott took
a weather class. The helmsmen took an intensive course that utilized Lasers (a particular
kind of one-person sailboat) to master boat
handling and improve driving skills.

Possibly the most intensive and time-
consuming course was taken by the crew's
medics, Jerry, Dave, George, and Mark. The
race rules required two crew members trained
as medics or a doctor onboard at all times.
The medics had to hold a recognized, current
(within two years), national first aid
certificate including cardiopulmonary resuscitation (CPR) and the Heimlich procedure
and be able to splint broken bones and apply
plaster casts, suture wounds, start intravenous
(IV) lines and give IV fluids, give both intra-
muscular and intravenous injections, open an
emergency airway through the neck to the
lungs, and apply temporary dental fillings.

With the help of his team of local physicians, Dr. Rudi trained *Chessie*'s medics. The
foursome attended medical lectures and took
skills labs, practicing on oranges, pigs, and,
eventually, each other. They learned to iden-
tify and evaluate problems, how to treat
them, and when to call for help. They stud-

Jerry Kirby, crew boss/
bowman/medic/me-
chanic, coached the
America 3 women's team
in the 1995 America's
Cup. For 34 years, Jerry
has sailed with top
skippers around the
world in both offshore
and inshore buoy races.

Greg Gendell, bowman, grew up sailing on the Magothy River (near Annapolis, Maryland) and turned his love of sailing into a career as both a sailmaker and a bowman. He was also in charge of food onboard *Chessie.* By eliminating individual packaging, he was able to cut down on weight and storage. A day's worth of food was put in a long plastic tube and labeled, with each meal separated and sealed, to prevent salt water from destroying it. The plastic bag was then used to store trash, since the fleet could not dispose of trash at sea.

ied the human body systems, such as the skeletal, muscular, and respiratory systems. They learned how to take someone's temperature and blood pressure and which medications should be given for which ailments, as well as how much and when. Perhaps most important, they learned how to communicate their findings to doctors on shore, who could be e-mailed or phoned for advice. With help days away, the medics had to be ready for every possibility, including those previous crews had experienced, such as resuscitation, hypothermia, shock, heart attack, broken bones, deep cuts, and puncture wounds. By the time *Chessie* left Southampton, her medics were prepared for the worst-case scenario.

Each boat was required to carry a copy of *The World Health Organisation International Medical Guide for Ships,* second edition, and identical first aid kits. Two splash-proof cases, along with the contents, would be supplied by the Race Committee; boats could add items if desired.

Roxanne Moore, a Baltimore nutritionist, volunteered her services to determine how many calories the sailors needed per day and what type and how much freeze-dried food would be packed for each leg. *Chessie* did not want to carry more food and weight than would be needed. Roxanne, in consultation with Dr. Rudi and Rob, determined that each sailor would burn an average of five thousand calories per day. Based on that assumption, she and Greg Gendell (who was in charge of safety and provisioning) developed a menu that would replace at least three thousand calories per day with breakfast, lunch, dinner, and a snack. For most of the legs, that was deemed sufficient.

In addition to a sailing crew, a shore crew was required. The shore crew would be responsible for repairing and restocking the boat; organizing travel, shipping, and accom-

Designed and outfitted by JT, the trailer served as a combination workshop and office.

John Thackwray ("JT"), who learned to sail on the Jersey Channel in England, now makes his home in Annapolis, Maryland.

modations; and the multitude of administrative tasks that accompanied a Whitbread effort. John Thackwray, known as JT to his friends, had been hired to design and outfit the team's two containers (the trailer part of a tractor trailer), which were donated by Living Classrooms Foundation trustee Ed Hale. Once outfitted, each container would serve as a combination workshop and office. The containers, equipped identically, would travel from port to port in a leap-frog manner. One would be shipped to Cape Town while the other was in use in Southampton, then the one in Southampton would be shipped directly to Fremantle, and so forth. JT, who has been involved in every aspect of sailing throughout his lifetime, became indispensable and joined the shore crew.

Bryan Fishback was retained as shore manager. He hired Jonathan Holstrom, a graduate of the Landing School and one of

Chessie's boatbuilders at Goetz, to travel to each port. Jon Patton, a sailor and recent college graduate, also joined the team. To keep the families together, some of the wives were hired. Sally Scott arranged travel and purchased uniforms, and Cary Swain became the office administrator. Suzy Nairn and Tucker Thompson, two local sailors, helped with prerace administration and odd jobs. With her crew relatively in place, *Chessie* was ready to be introduced to her already adoring fan club. She set sail for Baltimore/Annapolis and her christening.

On Friday, May 2, 1997, Pier Five in Baltimore's Inner Harbor was decked out for *Chessie's* christening. Over twelve hundred fans congregated for their first glimpse of the boat and crew that would soon be household names. The sleek, Spartan, high-tech yacht seemed to know she was the center of attention. Proudly flying her sponsors' flags and

Jon Patton ("JP") (*left*) and Bryan Fishback (*right*) stayed close to *Chessie* during a sail-testing exercise. Jon, who lives in Baltimore, has been a sailing instructor at Severn Sailing Association (Maryland), Beverly Yacht Club (Massachusetts), and Camp Robinhood (Maine). Bryan has worked for Farr as a naval architect and as a custom projects manager building offshore racing sailboats, including *Galicia Pescanova* (1993–94 Whitbread).

Jon Holstrom calls himself the "toy maker" because he makes big boys' toys. He sanded, drilled, painted, and patched *Chessie* around the world. His teammates and boatbuilders from other crews often sought his advice.

sporting her freshly applied graphics, *Chessie* bobbed gently at the end of the pier. Her preliminary sailing crew—Jim Allsopp, George Collins, Rick Deppe, Campbell Field, Mark Fischer, Greg Gendell, Tony Harmon, Jerry Kirby, Peter (Curt) Oetking, Christian Scherrer, Dave Scott, Grant Spanhake, Jonathan Swain, Paul van Dyke, and Juan Vila—talked to reporters and mingled with fans.

Chessie had indeed captured the hearts and imaginations of Marylanders and residents of the Chesapeake Bay region, students and professionals, sailors and nonsailors. For the next year, *Chessie* fans would become armchair adventurers as they watched *Chessie* circumnavigate the world. The race would be followed by television, radio, newspapers, magazines, and the Internet.

Sally and Dave Scott
found time to laugh
with a friend in Balti-
more. Sally, a native of
Baltimore, home-
schooled their son and
worked as shore crew
throughout the race.

Cary Swain, a native
Baltimorean who now
lives in Annapolis, has
worked closely with
Jono on his various
yachting campaigns.

Chessie waited patiently
for her christening.

CHRISTENING PARTICIPANTS

IN ADDITION TO *CHESSIE* AND HER CREW:

The Classic Catering People (hor d'oeuvres)

Ian Bailey-Wilmot, chairman of Whitbread Race
Committee

James Piper Bond, president of Living Classrooms
Foundation

George and Maureen Collins

Jed Drake, senior vice president of ESPN

DeHaven Hairston, graduate of Living Classrooms
Foundation

Mayor Al Hopkins, Annapolis

James Hunnicut (actor)

Gary Jobson, ESPN sailing commentator (master of
ceremonies)

Rev. P. Edward Kenny Jr.

Nikki Laws, Towson State University (soloist)

Linganore Winecellars (wine—Chessie's Legend)

Senator Barbara Mikulski

Senator Paul Sarbanes

Kathy Schmoke, daughter of Mayor Schmoke

Mayor Kurt Schmoke, Baltimore City

Towson State University Band (music)

Walbrook Maritime Academy Color Guard

David Winstead, secretary of the Department of
Transportation

Maureen Collins and
Kathy Schmoke, daugh-
ter of Mayor Schmoke,
broke a bottle of
Chessie's Legend over
the bow of the boat.
The wine was developed
by Linganore Wine-
cellars to celebrate
Maryland's entry in the
1997–98 Whitbread
Round the World Race.

More than twelve hundred staunch supporters congregated on Pier Five in Baltimore's Inner Harbor to meet *Chessie* and her crew.

With the water bubbling, *Chessie* the sea monster rose from the floor of the Inner Harbor. A creative team of teachers at the Living Classrooms Foundation had designed their own version of *Chessie,* complete with sunglasses.

The Living Classrooms Foundation Connection and the Whitbread Education Project

ROUND THE WORLD RACE
1997-98

For the first time in Whitbread history, a syndicate teamed with a non-profit. Never before had such a concept been tried, but George Collins had strong ties to the Living Classrooms Foundation and the missions of *Chessie Racing* and the Living Classrooms Foundation blended well. Since 1985, the foundation, using private-public partnerships, has built its programs on the concept that students, especially those needing extra guidance, placed in small classes (1:5 staff to student ratio) in challenging settings, respond to real-world applications of academics, career training, and life skills far more readily than they do in traditional classrooms. Participation has grown from a single program with one hundred students in 1985 (building the schooner *Lady Maryland*) to 40 programs (taking place aboard ships and ashore) with more than fifty thousand students a year. While elevating students' self-esteem and fostering multicultural exchange, the foundation's key objectives are cooperative learning, career development, and community service. *Chessie Racing* would

Left: Students learn the importance of teamwork while grinding *Chessie*'s huge sails. *Right:* Students plot the desired course onboard *Lady Maryland.*

be an ideal vehicle for academic lessons as well as life lessons like self-discipline, teamwork, goal setting, and perseverance.

What began rather simply with a handshake became a monumental endeavor, but one definitely worth the effort. While *Chessie Racing* was building a boat and crew, Living Classrooms Foundation was building a curriculum and its own crew. The Living Classrooms Foundation hired Bob Kendell and Sheryl Barr to develop the interdisciplinary curriculum and Christine Truett and Kathleen Hines to implement it.

The Living Classrooms Foundation Whitbread Education curriculum, designed to help teachers match state requirements through an interactive experience, directly connected classrooms to the nine-month world-class sailing adventure. It brought the world to students via two linked components: the "Ready to Race" unit and the

"*Chessie* Chase." The Ready to Race unit, a 10-lesson, 140-page curriculum, introduced students and teachers to the magic of the Whitbread through interdisciplinary, hands-on lessons for team teaching. The program combined such academic subjects as math, science, social studies, and language arts with Whitbread topics, such as weather, vessel design, navigation, and deep-water currents. In the *Chessie* Chase, students applied the lessons learned while participating in a virtual Whitbread Race on the foundation's worldwide website (www.livingclassrooms.org).

After six months, the program was almost ready. Living Classrooms Foundation brought in a group of 30 students to test it. Were the assignments easily understood? Was further explanation required? Did the program really capture the imaginations of the students? Would the students want to go back for more? Did the curriculum cover the required subject matter?

Students could follow
the race on the Living
Classrooms Foundation
website (www.living
classrooms.org).

The students prepared and tasted freeze-dried meals, learned the different sails and their purposes, and plotted courses from one port to the next. At the end of five weeks, Bob and Sheryl still had work to do, but they knew they were on the right track. The students loved it; they couldn't wait to go back to school so they could do the entire curriculum.

Participants in the Whitbread Race would have many daunting challenges to face. Each would be forced to master a variety of tasks, face many difficult decisions, and become familiar with foreign lands and seas. Success could only be attained through teamwork, skill, and ingenuity. The *Chessie* Chase participants would share these experiences, mastering tasks, making difficult decisions, and becoming familiar with the world.

The Whitbread Education Project curriculum had won over school administrators. More than 500 schools in 20 states and 7

foreign countries prepared their teachers and students to "chase" *Chessie* around the world. In August, the Living Classrooms Foundation held a workshop to show teachers how to turn their classroom into a boat and participate in the *Chessie* Chase. After Sheryl and Bob explained how the program worked, Kathy Alexander answered questions about the Whitbread Race, the crew, their training, and the boat. She described a day onboard *Chessie,* the lack of creature comforts, the jobs, the challenges, the camaraderie, the speed, and the thrill. Teachers took a physics lesson when they tried some of the hands-on activities. They attempted to build sailboats from clay, straws, and paper. Some stayed afloat. They snacked on freeze-dried food. No one asked for seconds. They surfed the Living Classrooms Foundation website and spent the afternoon sailing on the Chesapeake Bay aboard the *Lady Maryland,* a traditional schooner. Nonsailors discovered the

A Lesson for the EARTH SCIENCE or LANGUAGE ARTS teacher

5   Blowing in the Wind

Wind is air in motion relative to the rotating surface of the earth. According to Isaac Newton's Laws of Motion, the movement of air is the result of force imbalances. Sailing and using the wind for power requires developing an understanding of these principles. In the words of Joshua Slocum in <u>Sailing Alone Around The World</u>, "to know the laws that govern winds, and to know that you know them, will give you an easy mind..., otherwise you may tremble at the appearance of every cloud."

Sample Outcome and Skill Based Objectives

Science Outcomes
• Demonstrate the aquisition and integration of major concepts and unifying themes from the life, physical, and earth/space sciences

Writing Outcomes
• Writing for various audiences to inform - describing observations, and unifying concepts

Science Skills
• Formulate an operational definition
• Using explanatory models
• Theorizing

Writing Skills
• Recount an event in writing
• Write in response to experience
• Write in response to reading
• Structure an expository paragraph
• Structure a narrative (2 paragraphs)

Basic Ideas

• Temperature variation between land and sea causes air movement. Mountains absorb heat faster during daylight than nearby low areas, and lose heat faster at night.
• Air moves from regions of higher pressure to regions of lower pressure.
• There are different ways to measure wind speed.
• Winds can be calm, blow gently, steadily or move in rapid, destructive ways.
• Writing summaries is a way to organize and record information.

Additional Background Information

THE BEAUFORT SCALE

Force	MPH (KNOTS)*	Pressure Lbs./Sq.Ft.	Desc.	Wave Pattern	Wave Heights	Effects on Land	Small Cruiser
Force 1	1-3 (1-3)	.004-.036	Light Airs	Glassy calm, some ripples	Flat	Flag hangs limp, windvanes do not respond.	Use motor... Steerageway possible; full main and large drifter.
Force 3	8-12 (7-10)	.256-.576	Gentle breeze	Small glassy waves	.5-1'	Flag occasionally extends, leaves and twigs in constant motion.	Comfortable sailing. Noticeable heeling; full main and #1 genoa.
Force 5	19-24 (17-21)	1.44-2.30	Fresh breeze	Some whitecaps	1.5'-2.5'	Flag ripples, small leafy trees begin to sway.	Leeward rail near water. Single reef in main and #2 genoa.
Force 7	32-38 (28-33)	4.09-5.77	Moderate gale	Swells form with white-caps	4'-5.5'	Flag extended, whole trees in motion.	Progress to windward impossible. Three reefs in main and working jib.
Force 9	47-54 (41-47)	8.83-11.6	Strong gale	Waves begin to heighten and roll	7.5'-10'	Slight structural damage occurs.	Run under bare poles, lie ahull, or sit to sea anchor.

Note: Wind pressure varies greatly according to the shape of an object; pressures indicated are only approximate. Wave patterns are described for large open lakes or oceans. Smaller bodies of water will have diminished wave patterns. Also, wave patterns will be different near abrupt shore features like cliffs, or when the wind is blowing against a current. When judging waves, look into the wind to estimate their size and power, not downwind.

*MPH: Statute miles (5,280-feet) per hour. Used on inland waters.
KNOTS: Nautical miles (6,076-feet) per hour. Used at sea or on coastal waters.

49

Blowing in the Wind

parts of a sailboat and how they worked; sailors realized the difference between old, heavy boats and modern sailboats. But no one could fully comprehend the difference between the *Lady Maryland* and *Chessie Racing*. The *Lady Maryland* moves along at 6 knots, on a good day. *Chessie Racing* has clocked 32 knots.

By the beginning of the school semester, everyone was ready to go—except the Whitbread racers. The Whitbread Round the World Race did not begin until September 22. While the students studied the background materials, their excitement built. They studied their maps and prepared for their own journeys.

"As an avid sailor and schoolteacher in the Baltimore area," smiled Nancy Graham (teacher at McDonogh School), "I was excited to incorporate the Whitbread Race into my fourth grade curriculum. Ten boats, each made up of sailors from around the globe,

nine legs each to a different port, and *Chessie*—a hometown boat to follow. How exciting! All of our subjects tied in with the Whitbread theme, including literature.

"We began the year organizing working groups and picking boats to follow. We researched each boat for bio's on crew members, boat names, and country flags. We made a poster for each boat and researched past Whitbread races to talk about the dangers of the race," she said.

Although these students would not be able to sail on the W60s, they would be able to surf down giant seas on the Internet while planning sail changes and meeting navigational challenges with their classmates. Combining experience in adventure learning with leading-edge technology allowed the students to feel like they, too, were a part of the race.

Finally, the start day came. Covered by ESPN, the BBC, and others, the start was viewed worldwide. The next day students

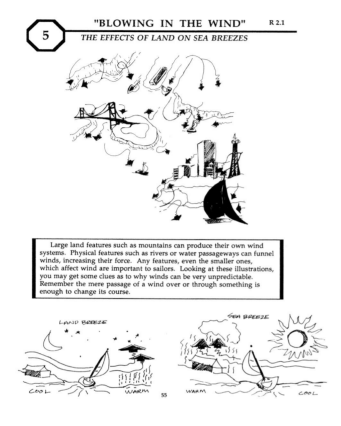

> Large land features such as mountains can produce their own wind systems. Physical features such as rivers or water passageways can funnel winds, increasing their force. Any features, even the smaller ones, which affect wind are important to sailors. Looking at these illustrations, you may get some clues as to why winds can be very unpredictable. Remember the mere passage of a wind over or through something is enough to change its course.

LAND BREEZE   SEA BREEZE

COOL   WARM   WARM   COOL   55

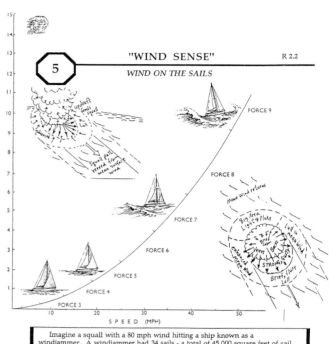

FORCE 9, FORCE 8, FORCE 7, FORCE 6, FORCE 5, FORCE 4, FORCE 3

SPEED (MPH) — 10 20 30 40 50

> Imagine a squall with a 80 mph wind hitting a ship known as a windjammer. A windjammer had 34 sails - a total of 45,000 square feet of sail. This awesome spread of sail soared more than 150 feet above the deck. If a 5mph breeze has 0.4 pounds per square inch of force on these sails, a 20 mph breeze has a 6.4 psf. Every time speed is increased by a factor of 4, the pressure on the sails multiplies 16 times. Can you figure out how many pounds of pressure would hit the windjammer if it ran into a squall with a wind speed of 80 mph in full sail? There are 144 square inches per square foot. Good luck!

56

came to school ready to begin the adventure of a lifetime.

"When the race began, we followed the updates, position reports, and news daily," explained Mrs. Graham. "We created our own bulletin board with a picture gallery and plotted their journey on a large laminated map that I purchased through Race Head-quarters. We kept a journal as each day passed and e-mailed the crew through the Living Classrooms Foundation program. When Kathy Alexander visited our classroom to share her role in the race, she brought sailor's gear for the children to try on. As a reward for the students' hard work, Parker Rockefeller arranged for skipper John Kostecki and navigator Juan Vila to talk with the children and give them a tour of the boat when the Whitbread came to town." She smiled. "The children were flying high with the excitement of such special attention."

As the race progressed, so did the *Chessie* Chase. At the end of each virtual leg, classes sent their completed assignments to Living Classrooms. Christine Truett and Kathleen Hines graded them and tallied up the scores. When the fleet sailed into Baltimore, the classes that had won a leg would have the opportunity to meet the *Chessie* crew at a special breakfast on April 24. Classes from North Chevy Chase Elementary School, Maryland; McDonogh School, Maryland; and John English School, Canada, won that privilege. The crew was showered with won-derful gifts—poems, banners, pictures—made by the students. The crew answered ques-tions, told stories about the Southern Ocean, the Doldrums, and foreign ports, and gave the students a personal tour of *Chessie*.

"Following the Whitbread brought my students and me very close. We shared a special bond and excitement that made learn-ing fun! We felt very connected to the whole

The *Chessie* crew enjoyed breakfast with the classes that had won a leg, or more, of the *Chessie* Chase.

event, especially with our involvement with the Living Classrooms," said Mrs. Graham.

Andy Mace, a student at the McDonogh School, explained his involvement. "It was neat. In Baltimore, we got to actually look all through *Chessie.* That was great, especially since we had been following her for so many months. *Brunel Sunergy* was the boat I was tracking. She tried hard but didn't win."

Another McDonogh student, Matt Mersky, said that "following the Whitbread was really interesting. Each day I wondered who would come in first and what their positions would be. We learned about a lot of cities on continents around the globe."

The entire crew of *Chessie* will remember the race and all of its harrowing experiences, the friends they met, the places they saw, but the most memorable experience will probably be the children, the e-mails they sent, and the look in their eyes when they finally met *Chessie* and her crew.

Staffed by 80 educators plus ship and museum personnel, the Living Classrooms Foundation currently operates a sailing maritime educational fleet consisting of the pungey schooner *Lady Maryland,* two skipjacks, and a Chesapeake Bay buyboat, as well as the Baltimore Maritime Museum's World War II submarine *Torsk,* Coast Guard cutter *Taney,* lightship *Chesapeake,* and a lighthouse built in 1856, a maritime institute, a marina, the Weinberg Education Center, the National Historic Seaport, and the Frederick Douglas–Isaac Myers Maritime Park. In addition to being recognized by the U.S. Department of Labor in 1996, 1997, and 1998 as one of the 18 most effective programs in the United States, the Living Classrooms Foundation received the Program of the Year award from the American Sail Training Association in 1995. James Piper Bond serves as CEO of the Living Classrooms Foundation, having taken the helm from founder Dennis O'Brien.

The Competition and the Scoring

Whitbread boats represented the United States, Britain, Holland, Monaco, Norway, and Sweden. Their crews came from around the world (New Zealand, 30; United Kingdom, 15; United States, 13; Holland, 12; Australia, 8; Sweden, 8; South Africa, 5; France, 4; Norway, 4; Canada, 2; Spain, 2; Switzerland, 2; Germany, 1; Italy, 1; and Ireland, 1), but they all shared one thing—a passion for sailing.

Because this elite group regularly competed on the world ocean racing circuit, most language and cultural barriers had already been overcome. In the close confines of a sailboat, crew members must accept one another's differences quickly if they want to win and stay on the circuit. For the most part, these sailors are self-employed contractors who are hired for a particular race. They must constantly look to the next race for continual employment. Despite their sailing prowess, if they cannot communicate with or easily accept others they probably will not be hired a second time.

America's Challenge

As Fuzz Spanhake explained, "*Chessie* was quite an international boat, with 10 Americans (George, Mark, Jerry, Whirly, Greg, Jim, Mike, Dee, John, and Tony), 2 Spaniards (Juan and Talpi), 2 Brits (Dave and Rick), 1 South African (Jono), and 3 Kiwis (Stu, Gavin, and me). The boat flew an American flag, the syndicate was headed by a very patriotic man (George), and it reflected the best qualities of America—a place for all nationalities to excel as one." Twelve sailors would crew each leg. As they lived, worked, and played together, they formed a cohesive unit.

Although each sailor was hired for a specific job, each had to master every job (except medic). At sea, situations could arise without warning, and there would be no time to teach a crew mate a new job. Storms, collisions, injuries, illnesses, breakdowns—Whitbread sailors have to be prepared *before* they go to sea.

Only one boat had a female crew—*EF Education* (Sail Number SWE 300000), skippered by Christine Guillou (France). Few women make it to this level of competition, whether because of lack of available jobs, inability to juggle family responsibilities, or a combination. Although some of the male sailors were married, with family joining them at various ports, *EF Education*'s crew was mostly single. One thing this crew definitely proved was that women are capable of competing at this level.

Sailors have always shared a special bond. No matter where they live or work, when sailors meet they instantly bond with one another, speaking the same sailing jargon, moving at the same pace, and enjoying the same things. They are family. At the Whitbread level of competition, the sailors are a very close-knit family.

They share several attributes, including extreme competitiveness, passion for the sport, desire and willingness to challenge their limits, and superb skill. Although these attributes exist in all professional athletes, the event differentiates the Whitbread athletes from others. The race requires its participants to share nine straight months of their lives. There are no breaks. Even when the individual crews are separated by miles of ocean, they are still closer to one another than to the rest of the human race. In fact, during Leg 5, the Whitbread fleet passed the point considered farthest from civilization. The distances are long and the territory traversed is dangerous and lonely.

When trouble strikes, the closest possible help is the competition. The crews respect and trust one another. They know that if they call for assistance at sea the other boats will come to their aid. Because the crews are self-reliant, that call seldom rings out; when it does, it is answered immediately. This is unique to yacht racing, especially the Whit-

Top: EF Education

Bottom: EF Language

bread, where the crews are alone with their competition. In the 1989–90 Whitbread, *Martela's* (Finland) keel came loose. In 15 seconds, the boat capsized. Somehow the crew scrambled to the inverted hull and was then rescued by *Merit Cup* (Switzerland). In the 1993–94 Whitbread, *Brooksfield* (Italy) was reported missing in the Southern Ocean. *La Poste* (France) and *Winston* (United States) discovered the boat and crew safe; however, the rudder had broken and caused the stern to fill with icy water, submerging the communication equipment. The crew finally stuffed a bucket in the hole and continued sailing. Although the competition is avid, your competition is also your ally.

The fierce competition is demonstrated in the syndicates' budgets. Making the boat go faster can be a never-ending process if the funds are available. Corporate sponsorship is a must. In fact, the only syndicate without

corporate backing was *Chessie Racing*. Because the budgets are so high, syndicates often have multiple corporate sponsors. Like NASCAR, the boats become billboards with multiple logos plastering the hull, the sails, and the deck. The budget must cover boat design; boat building (material and labor); sail development; salaries for skipper, crew, and shore crew; gear; food, both on and off the water; housing; travel; miscellaneous expenses; and unforeseen emergencies.

The nationality of the boat usually reflects the nationality of the leading corporate sponsor or the syndicate organizer. For instance, Dennis Conner (United States) was the syndicate organizer and the driving force behind *Toshiba;* therefore, *Toshiba* represented the United States. Yet the EF boats, whose corporate sponsors were from Sweden, represented Sweden, even though their skippers were from the United States and France. Although

Merit Cup

the Whitbread Race was relatively new to the United States, three syndicates represented it: *America's Challenge* (Sail Number USA 11), *Chessie Racing* (Sail Number USA 60), and *Toshiba* (Sail Number USA 1).

Chessie and *America's Challenge* were built by Goetz Custom Boats. These were the only two syndicates to use a common boatbuilder. Each boat had a separate construction team, with the boats housed behind large curtains to protect design secrets. All employees and everyone who visited the complex had to sign a confidentiality statement; photographs had to be approved.

Being a one-design fleet, the similarities between boats were numerous and the differences few. Only two boats were not Farr-designed boats. *America's Challenge* was designed by Alan Andrews; *Brunel Sunergy* (Sail Number NED 11), which sailed for Holland,

was designed by Judel Vrolijk. Still, there were differences between the Farr boats.

The crew and sailmakers for *EF Language* (Sail Number SWE 13000) developed the whomper sail (the huge sail measured as a spinnaker). They knew that, if they were to use it for the race, the boat would require more stability and a reinforced mast. As a result, the syndicate's boats (*EF Language* and *EF Education*) were a little more conservative, offering more stability, and their masts were reinforced before the race. Lawrie Smith, who was the original skipper for *EF Language* and who initiated development of the whomper sail, had *Silk Cut*'s (Great Britain—Sail Number GBR 1) mast reinforced, too. If the new sail passed inspection, they wanted to be ready.

Another more noticeable difference in design appeared in the keels. *America's Challenge,* the EF boats, *Merit Cup* (Monaco—Sail Number MON 700)*, Silk Cut,* and

Toshiba chose a T-shaped keel. *Brunel Sunergy, Chessie, Innovation Kvaerner* (Norway—Sail Number NOR 2), and *Swedish Match* (Sweden—Sail Number SWE 2000) opted for the L-shaped keel.

The use of training boats contributed heavily to the success of the syndicates. *Brunel Sunergy* and *Toshiba* had no training boats of record, but Dennis Conner (*Toshiba*) had raced *Winston* (W60) in the previous race. *Chessie* used a Corel 45, which could accommodate a crew of 12 men. *America's Challenge* used a first-generation W60, and the rest of the fleet used 1993–94 Whitbread veterans. EF used *Intrum Justitia,* which had broken the monohull record, and *Galicia Pescanova. Innovation Kvaerner* bought *Winston* for training; *Merit Cup* used *Merit Cup 2. Silk Cut* opted for *Reebok/Dolphin & Youth,* while *Swedish Match* purchased *Heineken* and *Tokio.*

The roles of skipper and navigator are very demanding in the Whitbread Race. Previous Whitbread experience is almost a prerequisite for those positions. In fact, 80 percent of the sailors had previously sailed in the Whitbread. However, *Brunel Sunergy* (Hans Bouscholte), *Chessie, EF Education* (Christine Guillou), and *EF Language* (Paul Cayard) chose skippers without Whitbread experience. *America's Challenge* (Ross Fields), *Merit Cup* (Grant Dalton), *Silk Cut* (Lawrie Smith), and *Toshiba* (Chris Dickson/Dennis Conner) chose skippers who had skippered in prior Whitbreads. The skippers of *Innovation Kvaerner* (Knut Frostad) and *Swedish Match* (Gunnar Kranz) had done the Whitbread but not as skippers. Whitbread experience would prove handy, but their ability to bind a team into a fighting unit would prove even more valuable. *Chessie Racing* was the only syndicate to rotate her skippers, although *Toshiba*

and *Brunel Sunergy* changed skippers midstream. Only *EF Education*'s and *Brunel Sunergy*'s navigators lacked Whitbread experience.

In Southampton before the race, the Whitbread crews were politely wary of one another, eyeing their competition with a mixture of respect and concern. Most of the sailors had either raced with or against one another. Three skippers had sailed together in the last Whitbread onboard *Intrum Justitia*—Lawrie Smith, Knut Frostad, and Gunnar Krantz. Paul Standbridge (*Toshiba*) had also sailed with them. They had raced against skippers Grant Dalton, Ross Fields, Chris Dickson, and Dennis Conner. The sailors knew one another, and they knew one another's strengths and weaknesses. What they didn't know was the strengths and weaknesses of one another's boats and the unity of the crews—those details remained within the confines of one's own crew. Everyone had their eyes on the same prize, winning the 1997–98 Whitbread Round the World Race.

As the race progressed, the crews learned the strengths and weaknesses of the other boats, as well as their own. The wariness progressively dispersed, but the competitiveness never dissipated. While they kept team secrets to themselves, the lifelong friendships they built stretched across the entire fleet. By the time they returned to Southampton, they were one big family.

For the first time, the Whitbread used a point system, awarding each yacht points for the position in which it finished. In prior races, the accumulated time had determined the winner. Now the yacht with the most points would win. Each leg was assigned a set of points based on its length and difficulty. The first three yachts to finish would receive bonus points (5, 2, and 1, respectively).

Where E equals the number of boats starting the race and LSC equals the assigned value for the appropriate leg, the formula is:

$$(E \times LSC) + 5 = \text{First Place}$$
$$[(E - 1) \times LSC] + 2 = \text{Second Place}$$
$$[(E - 2) \times LSC] + 1 = \text{Third Place}$$
$$[(E - 3) \times LSC] = \text{Fourth Place, and so on}$$

LSC for Leg 1 = 12
LSC for Leg 2 = 12
LSC for Leg 3 = 10
LSC for Leg 4 = 10
LSC for Leg 5 = 13
LSC for Leg 6 = 11
LSC for Leg 7 = 10
LSC for Leg 8 = 11
LSC for Leg 9 = 10

The winner would not receive a monetary prize. Instead, glory, respect, fame, and a sense of accomplishment were awarded the winning crew; however, in a race like the Whitbread, everyone who competes should be considered a winner.

The first three boats for each leg would receive a silver platter. In addition, the yacht "covering the greatest distance in a 24-hour period" would win a silver platter, and media prizes would be given to the crews who produced the best video, still pictures, and e-mails for each leg.

Southampton, England, to Cape Town, South Africa

LEG 1

DISTANCE
7350 nautical miles

START DATE
September 21, 1997

ESTIMATED ARRIVAL DATE
October 22, 1997

Yachting overpowered Southampton during September 1997. In addition to the annual Southampton Boat Show, 10 crews geared up for the start of the 1997–98 Whitbread Round the World Race. Reporters and press officers scurried around trying to secure interviews, while crews dodged them to spend the last few hours with family or boat. *Silk Cut,* sailing for Britain, garnered the most attention. The press room, a tent on a converted parking lot, buzzed. Tandem and CompuServe consultants bounced from problem to problem as reporters struggled to file their stories before deadlines.

As the weeks progressed, the tension level increased exponentially. The Fastnet Race is a world circuit yacht race (600 nautical miles) that takes place in August of every odd-numbered year. It starts at Cowes, England (the Isle of Wight), circles Fastnet Rock in the Irish Sea (the southern tip of Ireland), and finishes at Plymouth, England. The Fastnet had given the crews an opportunity to see each other in action. There

Young sailors "at work"

were also some crew changes throughout the fleet. From *Chessie,* Curt Oetking moved to *EF Language,* and Campbell Fields decided to sail with his father, Ross Fields, onboard *America's Challenge.* With the boats lined up next to one another, the crews studied and evaluated their competition at a distance, trying to discover each other's strengths and weaknesses. Everyone seemed to have too many last minute jobs, and time was running out. As rumors circulated, British bookmakers posted new odds hourly. Was *Toshiba* underweight? Would Nick White leave *EF Language* to join *America's Challenge*?

With the families there to see the sailors off, children scurried around, constantly underfoot and growing louder by the day. In fact, *Chessie* had more than its share of family members in Southampton for the start. In addition to spouses and parents, 11 children under the age of eight skipped around the *Chessie* compound, each trying to be "one of

the guys." They sorted nuts and bolts, helped carry sails, delivered sandwiches, entertained the youngest children, and, of course, decorated the container and apartments with their artwork and toys.

As this junior sailing team shadowed their fathers from container to boat and back again, they captured the hearts and attention of everyone, including the press corps. It was not long before *Chessie* was nicknamed "the kids' boat." With the Living Classrooms Foundation connection, Kathy made sure the name stuck.

Despite the accompanying chaos, somehow everything got done. The boats and sails were measured, and all passed the strict scrutiny of the measurers. Linda Jones, the recently hired team chef, who balanced her careers between crewing in international regattas and freelance cooking on luxury charter yachts, prepared and packed one last meal for the crew. After that, reconstituted

Linda Jones, team chef, grew up in Connecticut and was introduced to sailing in the late seventies.

CREW FOR CHESSIE RACING

LEG

1

Jim Allsopp, coskipper/tactician

Mark Fischer, coskipper

Juan Vila, navigator

Grant "Fuzz" Spanhake, watch captain

Dave Scott, watch captain/sailmaker

Jerry Kirby, crew boss/bowman

Rick Deppe, bowman

Greg Gendell, bowman

Antonio "Talpi" Piris, trimmer/driver

Paul "Whirly" van Dyke, trimmer/driver

Jonathan "Jono" Swain, trimmer/driver

Stu Wilson, grinder/sailmaker

freeze-dried food would provide their nourishment for the next 30+ days. Packed and finally ready to leave the dock, all that remained were the good-byes, and there were plenty. Rick Deppe had to say good-bye to his wife by phone. She had stayed in Annapolis, Maryland, to give birth to their second child.

Leg 1 of the race would sail from Southampton, England, to Cape Town, South Africa. Because of political bans, an international race had not stopped in South Africa for 17 years.

For the start of the legs, each boat could invite up to three guests; however, the guests were forbidden to help in any way except as rail meat (sitting on the side of the boat to add ballast or weight). Usually, reporters and photographers occupied the guest slots, but *Chessie* saved at least two for family. For Leg 1, *Chessie* invited George Collins, who chose not to sail this leg; his son, David; and Andrew Hurst, reporter for *Seahorse,* an international yachting magazine.

The 10 W60s left the dock in alphabetical order to the sounds of their countries' national anthems or their theme songs. As *Chessie* pulled away from the dock, the *Chessie* kids yelled "good-bye Daddy" and then broke into a chant of "*Chessie, Chessie,*" bringing smiles and tears to the thousands of spectators lining the walls at Race Village.

The start of the Whitbread has become an event in itself—a carnival on water. While the yachts made their way to the Solent (a strait of the English Channel between mainland England and the Isle of Wight), families maneuvered through the crowds to find their spectator boat. Excitement grew as the 100-foot powerboat *Chessie* had chartered motored out and positioned herself downwind of the starting line to provide the 50+ family members a front-row seat. Suddenly, the show began. The Red Arrows (the United

Top: The fleet split up, with some hugging the shore to avoid the foul tide and some figuring on more wind away from the shore. *Bottom:* With her Code 3 reaching spinnaker, *Chessie* maneuvered her way through the spectator fleet.

Kingdom's version of the Blue Angels) streaked through the air, putting on a spectacular show of daredevil flying and leaving everyone in awe. At the 10-minute gun, a half-dozen or more helicopters and a blimp positioned themselves to photograph the start. The yachts circled the area, planning their approach to the starting line. *Chessie* maneuvered under her main and jib before hoisting her Code 3 reaching spinnaker (*reaching spinnaker*—a large, billowing headsail used when the wind is coming across the boat from the back). Under bright, sunny skies, the start gun sounded on time and the boats were off. As Jono recalled, "I'm sure you've all heard about our hectic trip down the Solent. Well, luckily the 15–18 knots of breeze and favorable current shot us out past the Needles [rock formation at the tip of the Solent] and into the English Channel."

"We passed Hurst Castle in fourth place. Unfortunately, we chose the wrong sail and

dropped *Chessie* into sixth place. This is going to be one very close race. One bad spinnaker peel and we lose two boat lengths," the crew's e-mail read.

EF Language hoisted her Code 0—the whomper—and changed the complexion of the race. Most of the fleet had experimented with such a sail and knew its capabilities but not how it had passed measurement inspection. The other boats had given up developing the sail early in their campaign because of the measurement rules. How had Cayard (*EF Language*) gotten approval? And, more important, how soon could the other syndicates make one? As *EF Language* sailed away, the rest of the fleet looked on helplessly—except to e-mail their shore crew with the urgent request, "Get us a Code 0!"

The spectator fleet stayed with the W60s as long as it could. Eventually turning back, *Chessie*'s shore crew returned to Southampton. Some headed for the "Thank God

Left: Mark Fischer guided *Chessie* through the spectator fleet while the crew stayed alert for needed maneuvers. *Bottom:* Prepared for a very wet ride, the press corps tried to keep up with the fleet.

They're Gone" party (a party held after each restart for the shore crews to celebrate getting the boats finished in time), while others drifted to their computers to check the fleet's progress. Repacking and preparing the containers for shipping was the task scheduled for the following morning. The main container (the traveling workshop ladened with all the tools, the chase boat, and a boat trailer) had to be shipped to Fremantle, Australia. (An identical one was waiting for the crew in Cape Town, South Africa.) The much smaller air-freight container, piled high with suitcases and Linda's cooking tools, had to be packed for Cape Town.

"After a pretty eventful first few hours, namely, a broken halyard [line used to hoist sails] and a broken top-mast backstay shackle [metal coupler used to attach sails], the breeze started to die and swing aft," remembered Jono. "The first week or so out, the

Jonathan "Jono" Swain,
trimmer/driver/rigger/
alternate cameraman,
was looking forward to
sailing back home to
South Africa. Frustrated
by the years of political
bans against all sports,
he had moved to the
United States in 1990.
A versatile sailor
and superb driver, he
has since moved up
the ranks in the sailing
community.

positions changed frequently on the leader board [the position update that told the crews how they were doing compared to their opponents], as everyone was positioning themselves in anticipation of the high pressure that was moving eastward toward Portugal and Spain. One night in particular, we surfed parallel to *Toshiba*. They were about three miles to leeward [the side away from the wind], when suddenly they headed up, took our transom [back of the boat], and ended up to weather of us [side where the wind was coming from]. The next day we watched as they blew out two sails in succession. That was the last we would see of them."

The crews were asked to send daily e-mails describing the sailing, which would be posted on the website. *Chessie Racing*'s e-mail for Wednesday, September 24, 1997, 15:27:55: "Light air, moderate temperatures, and partly

Chessie's shore crew packed and unpacked the containers at each stopover.

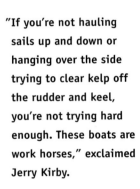

"If you're not hauling sails up and down or hanging over the side trying to clear kelp off the rudder and keel, you're not trying hard enough. These boats are work horses," exclaimed Jerry Kirby.

cloudy skies," wrote Mark. "In the old days of wooden ships and iron men, the crew just needed to be able to hoist the sails and tie good knots. The sails still need to go up and down, and there are still knots to tie, but instead of spending idle time whittling scrimshaw, today's crews need to be electricians, plumbers, riggers, composite experts, diesel mechanics, and computer scientists just to keep the boat running. Throw in a weatherman and a cameraman and you have a miniature version of modern-day technical society.

"It has actually been an easy race so far, and still we've managed to break a halyard, a stanchion leg [support at the edge of the deck that holds the lifelines], and a running backstay shackle [coupler attached to the permanent rigging at the back of the boat]. We've also had to rewire our 12-volt system and rebuild our ballast system, and we're still

working on our generator motor because it's barely running. To boot, we can't get the video editing system to work, and I don't think the digital still camera output is working very well either. I would swear to our shore team we've been careful, but they would probably just scoff at the idea.

"The guys just go about the business of their maintenance and repair tasks with a jovial and workmanlike attitude. It's no big deal to have two full repair jobs laid out above and below deck simultaneously. At the same time, the kettle is whistling, the bowman is going up the mast for a spinnaker peel [sail change], and the other bowman has the video camera rolling."

Rick Deppe, usually carefree and easy going, had not been himself. An e-mail from home snapped him out of it. "The best news came this morning when Race Headquarters told us Rick had become a father for the second time last night at 9:00 P.M. Today we have a very happy ship," wrote Fuzz. Maureen e-mailed a picture of the baby to *Chessie* and informed the crew that "she is perfect except she seems to have her father's hairline."

It was not long before the crew lost track of the days. Greg's menu served as the crew's calendar, tracking how long they had been at sea, and gave the boys an idea of what they were eating. "Freeze-dried food is all mush; it just comes in different colors" was a common complaint among the sailors. Jerry Kirby described one breakfast as "Bandito Scramble, a fine mélange of disposal drippings seasoned with a hint of arsenic and battery acid and a strong finish reminiscent of garden fertilizer. This fine dish finds its name from the chef, 'Pancho' Juan Vila, who actually eats extra helpings of this all-time culinary stinker."

On board *Chessie,* the crew had settled into its routine. "We had *Silk Cut* in sight for what seemed like an eternity but was probably only five days in total. This provided us good motivation as it kept us focused every hour we were on watch. We were running an overlapping 'Swedish watch' system, which is four hours on, four hours off at night, when seeing and driving are tougher, and six on, six off during the day," said Jono.

As the fleet made its way through the Atlantic, Dalton (*Merit Cup*) complained of the "crap floating around." Krantz (*Swedish Match*) had to stop the boat to clear the rudder of plastic, sending her to the back of the fleet. Icebergs were not a threat in these waters; lost shipping containers were. "Every year thousands of shipping containers are lost over the side of cargo ships. Containers up to 40 feet long float around for hours or days, until they fill with water and sink," explained Emily Robertson, reporter for Quokka

Sports, which developed and ran the website. The sailors stayed alert.

The fleet of W60s were so evenly matched that, after a week of racing, *Silk Cut* and *Chessie* were still in a jibing duel (turning the stern through the wind). "Only a few miles apart, matching each other gybe for gybe [jibe], day and night. So far the intensity level hasn't dropped a notch since we left Southampton. With 6,000 nautical miles [one nautical mile is equal to 6,076 feet, or one minute of the earth's latitude] to go, it will be interesting to see how long this intensity will last," *Chessie*'s daily e-mail read.

As the fleet neared the equator, the temperatures rose. Sleeping was difficult enough with the motion of the boat at high speed and the rudder humming at high pitch. Now, it was unbearable: "120° temperatures were not uncommon inside the boat, and neither was having your watch-mate in the bunk

Rick Deppe ate his breakfast but didn't ask for seconds.

of the mast brought terrific footage and some useful practice administering first aid under sail. While cameraman Rick Deppe perched at the top of the mast (85 feet above the deck), filming Jerry Kirby being hoisted to the top, *Chessie* swayed as she surfed through some 10-foot arcs. Rick, still at the top of the mast, lost his grip, crashed into the rig, and sustained a cut to his forehead. While the film continued rolling, Jerry, one of the team's medics, cleaned and bandaged Rick's wounds.

El Niño played havoc with the fleet. The weather did not imitate that of previous races, which had been the basis of much boat and sail development. After extensive discussion, Jim, coskipper/tactician, and Juan Vila, navigator, opted to sail between the Cape Verde islands. It was a gutsy move. Would there be wind, or would *Chessie* be blanketed by the mountains' shadows? "Large, majestic mountains sat upon a barren volcanic landscape. Cinder-block buildings dotted the shore. It was nice to see land again, but it wasn't the land we were all looking forward to," said Jono. The game plan worked and they sailed through, saving a few hours.

It was not long before *Chessie* was caught in a high-pressure system and crept toward the Doldrums. Concern grew that this leg might take longer than originally estimated, possibly 35 days instead of 33 days. Would the food and fuel last? *Chessie* had packed food for 35 days, but with weight at such a premium, she carried only the minimum amount of fuel to make it to Cape Town. If the fuel ran out, the crew would be without water or power to run the ballast system or electronics, so fuel rationing commenced. Other crews, who had packed food for 32 or 33 days, began rationing food as well.

On Day 13, Fuzz e-mailed: "It's now 2:25 A.M. Sleep is impossible; it's so *hot*. There is no air circulation, the motion of the boat is

above you sweating down on top of you," grimaced Jono. The crew's aroma had risen considerably. Fuzz chuckled, "Jim Allsopp had smuggled a bar of saltwater soap on board, and it became communal property. A bath consisted of one bucket of saltwater over the head, soap up quickly, and rinse with one more bucket. After a week of not washing, it was pure luxury."

Exciting sailing, constant sail changes, repairs, and long hours peppered the fleet's daily e-mails. "Is all our hard work going to be enough?" asked Stu Wilson. "What are the other boats in the fleet doing right now?" The watch going off duty delayed sleep until it received the position report to see how it had done. The position reports arrived every six hours. In addition to competing against the other boats, the watches competed against each other.

Filming a spinnaker change from the top

Appreciated but not envied, Rick Deppe, Jerry Kirby, and Greg Gendell, *Chessie*'s bowmen, had one of the least favorite and most treacherous jobs on the boat. They had to go to the top of the mast for sail changes and tangled lines. The whiplash at the top of the rig is enormous in heavy air and even worse in light air, when the seas take over the motion.

Sailing in the tropics

so violent, and I have a headache so dehydration must be setting in. I need to drink more, but we are on water rations because this leg looks like it will take 3 or 4 days longer than anticipated because of light air. This means we are conserving fuel, which means running our water maker less."

As the wind picked up, crew morale improved. "We are absolutely flying right now. The gunwale [the edge of the deck] of the boat is in the water, spray flying off the leeward sidestays [the standing rigging on the side of the boat] and pouring into the cockpit," Fuzz e-mailed. "The adrenaline is pumping through the veins of the crew as the informal competition among the guys, to beat their crew mates' top speed, gets into full swing. We gotta catch more waves! It's hard to believe that in 10 hours we may be becalmed in the Doldrums. It doesn't seem possible for *Chessie* to slow down."

Chessie finally arrived at the Doldrums but not as expected. With huge rain clouds, lightning, thunder, and wind swinging wildly with every cloud, the crew was put to the test again. Still within sight of *Silk Cut,* the two crews tried everything for that little bit of extra speed. "Jib up, no change that, spinnaker up; no, let's try the jib again" was the typical conversation on deck. The water ballast system was in constant use, as *Chessie* tried to beat the wind and *Silk Cut.* Unfortunately, it also consumed two and a half days worth of fuel. "One more day of this and we definitely won't make it to Cape Town with enough fuel," reported Fuzz.

Brunel Sunergy hit a whale while doing about 10 knots and lost 50 centimeters of her rudder. Fortunately, there was no leakage. Could her crew continue sailing, or would it have to find a harbor to repair the rudder? It was not long before Bouscholte, the skipper, decided that *Brunel* had to put in for repairs. The rudder could not take the pressure anticipated in rough seas at the speeds necessary to compete. She limped into Recife, in the northeastern part of Brazil, for repairs.

Flying fish plagued the fleet. "One hit Justin in the side of the head last night at about 25 miles per hour," wrote Cayard (*EF Language*). As Chris Dickson (*Toshiba*) wrote, "Shirt off and all concentration, wind about 15 knots and boat speed about 12 when WHACK. I was punched in the face by a rather aggressive flying fish doing 20 knots in the opposite direction; left me close to seeing stars of the nongalactic type. A black eye and bruised eyeball were soon forgotten, but the fishy smell has taken a little longer to get rid of." With food being rationed and no restocking while making repairs, one of *Brunel*'s crew turned the flying fish into sushi.

The equator, the imaginary line separating the Northern and Southern Hemispheres, is revered by sailors. Their folklore tells of King Neptune, god of the seas, visiting sailors the first time they cross that imaginary line and passing judgment for any onboard crimes. To soften the punishments, sailors hold an elaborate celebration when crossing the equator to welcome King Neptune. Typically, one of the experienced crew members (who has crossed the equator) dresses up as King Neptune and passes judgment on the virgin crew members (those who have not crossed the equator before). Punishments usually consist of eating disgusting mixtures of leftover food and being smeared with grunge from the bilge.

At 12:30 P.M. on Day 16 (October 8), *Chessie* reached the equator, and King Neptune, played by Talpi Piris, held court. He ceremoniously dished "kitchen muck" over the equator virgins of the crew: Dave, Greg, Stu, Rick, Mark, and Whirly. Jerry made an offering of *Chessie*'s valued "Skandi Shake Mix" in the hope that King Neptune and the wind gods would grant *Chessie* favorable winds throughout her journey.

The offering must have worked. It was not long before *Chessie* was moving again. Passing the dry, barren De Fernando de Noronaha Islands, 186 miles off the coast of Brazil, the crew spotted a swordfish jumping about a hundred feet off their beam. "We are slamming into head seas because the wind lifts us and, instead of being at a comfortable angle to the waves, we get them almost directly head on," e-mailed Fuzz. "Down below the slamming sounds a lot worse than on deck. There are many stern looks from below as people get bounced, literally, out of their bunks."

Various sailors described sailing a W60. Dickson (*Toshiba*) may have summed it up best, "Silence . . . Bang! Crash! Swoosh! Splash! Shudder. Shudder. Shudder! This is

HALFWAY RESULTS

	BOAT	NAUTICAL MILES TO LEADER	LEG
1	*Innovation Kvaerner*	0.0	
2	*Merit Cup*	18.8	
3	*EF Language*	32.9	
4	*Silk Cut*	139.8	
5	*Chessie Racing*	152.8	
6	*Toshiba*	336.5	
7	*America's Challenge*	364.2	
8	*Swedish Match*	400.5	
9	*EF Education*	558.3	
10	*Brunel Sunergy*	568.7	

1

the noise that happens about five times a minute as we bang our way upwind. The silence is the boat being launched at 10 knots out of a wave going 20 knots in the other direction. Bang—as the boat lands on solid water in the trough on the other side. Crash—as the bow buries deeper into the ocean ahead. Swoosh—as tons of water are thrown sideways and up. Splash—as some of that water lands on the foredeck, the cockpit, mast, sails, and crew; then shuddering throughout the entire boat—as the shock waves ripple backward and forward for five seconds or so, and then silence. It all happens again and again," he explained.

Fuzz, the designated e-mailer, grew weary of his task. The crew decided that each member would take a turn writing about his experience. "It has been a rather long leg so far," wrote Whirly van Dyke. "Although it doesn't take the same type of concentration to sail the boat well in these lighter conditions as it does when it is blowing thirty, it is just as mentally demanding. Trying to squeeze every tenth of a knot [one nautical mile per hour] of speed out of the boat under a scorching tropical sun is very difficult. On the other hand, when we are lying on our side pulling the remnants of the heavy spinnaker out of the water and peeling the boom [the permanent spar to which the mainsail is attached] off the running backstays [the standing rigging at the back of the boat], we will be thinking of how nice and pleasant it is sailing in the tropics." Then, as an afterthought, he pondered, "There is a long way to go, and I have had the same t-shirt on for 20 days. I wonder if I will wear it to the finish?"

Stu, taking his turn, wrote that, "as sailmaker onboard *Chessie,* so far my work load has been light. As fate would have it, last night as I lay in my bunk trying to think of what I was going to write about, I suddenly knew. I could hear the on-deck watch peeling

sails, and from the conversation I knew the new sail was the Code 1. As the sail set, I heard a voice say, 'The wind speed has gone up, and we are not making course.' I felt the boat heel a little more than desired, and the cry came for water in the ballast tanks. 'Oh boy!' I thought, 'the boys are pushing it again.' As I felt the water come in and the boat speed climb, I started to relax, almost falling asleep. Just then, 'BANG!' and I was pushed back into the ballast tank wall as the boat bolted upright under the relieved load off the broken sail. Bodies quickly climbed on deck, recovered the old sail, and set the replacement. That was the end of my sleep as I gathered the sail repair kit, set up the sewing machine, and started repairing the damage."

Becalmed again, *Chessie* drifted near the island of Trinidade. "We ended up sitting off that damn island for the best part of 40 hours," remembered Jono. "Somebody from the island actually radioed us to ask why we were hanging around." While becalmed, a few Chessians dove in for a refreshing swim and took advantage of the opportunity to wipe down the bottom of the boat, removing growth that had accumulated during the 21 days of sailing. After the swimmers climbed back in the boat, Greg spotted a shark. "He was trying to sneak up on us," he chuckled, "but his dorsal fin coming out of the water blew his cover." Pilot whales and jellyfish also investigated the drifting boat.

During these slow periods, the crew entertained each other with stories and discussed philosophies of life. Greg decided that his e-mail would be a list of the Top Ten Non-Sailing-Related Topics onboard *Chessie Racing:* "(10) personal hygiene—is it really worth it? (9) debates as to whether or not it is hotter than 40 hells; (8) unanswered questions about flying fish; (7) the flora and fauna of the South Atlantic coasts; (6) Stu Wilson's

REPAIRING SAILS WHILE SAILING

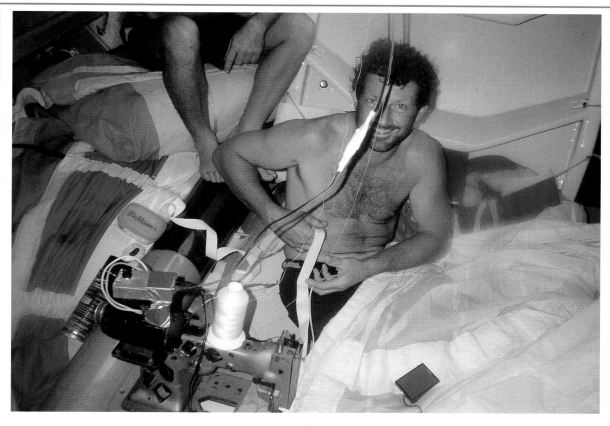

Dave repaired the sails below deck.

Ideally, sails do not rip or blow out, or they are repaired when the boat is docked. Unfortunately, in the extreme conditions of the Whitbread, life is far from ideal. With the limited onboard sail inventory, ripped sails often had to be repaired while the boat was slicing through the water or bouncing off waves.

Because the lighter sewing machine did not hold up, *Chessie* had a metal one onboard. The crew would drag the ripped sail down below while Dave and Stu (*Chessie*'s sailmakers) would often strap mining headlamps on for light. "Acetone and adhesive were sprayed on the sail to remove the salt. Then 3-inch-wide Dacron sticky tape was applied, front and back, to bind the torn edges. The Dacron sticky tape was then sewn to the sail, with up to three rows on each side of the tear. This procedure could take up to 5 hours," Dave explained. "Ninety-nine percent of our onboard repairs were 'downwind' sails," Dave calculated.

"Sometimes we got lucky. We were close enough to the next stopover and could wait to repair the sails," he smiled. "Most of the stopovers had a sail loft nearby, but we had to work at night after normal production was finished because of limited loft floor space. Brazil did not have a loft. *Chessie, Toshiba, Merit Cup,* and *Silk Cut* had to set up camp in an old, converted bowling alley to repair sails. It was the only building in town large enough to house the sails."

Spray adhesive glued the Dacron tape to the mainsail.

Chessie, totally be-calmed, drifted near Trinidade.

world tour of lager sampling; (5) the picture above our galley of the Spice Girls; (4) endless running commentary of stories and jokes from Jerry Kirby; (3) questions, comments, and concerns about the delicious masterpieces put out from our galley; (2) lawn maintenance and landscaping of the professional sailor; (1) the NFL."

Finally, the breeze filled in and *Chessie* sped toward Cape Town. A front moved through, producing some pretty good surfing conditions, and the crew pulled out the foul weather gear. "Although the pressure was pretty much off, as *Silk Cut* had moved 150 miles ahead and *Toshiba* and *America's Challenge* were 100+ miles behind, we had a taste of W60 conditions at their best: 35 knots up the butt with a Code 4 spinnaker up," remembered Jono.

During this sleigh ride, Jerry was sent aloft to transfer some halyards and commented on

his impressions. "Looking into the darkness, with spray flying everywhere, I looked down toward the cockpit and saw Fuzz in the red glow of the binnacle [the on-deck instrument panel], dialing [steering] into another South Atlantic roller. The mast rolled to leeward as he steered the boat high. Just when it seemed we would broach [lay the boat on its side], the water ballast kicked in. Fuzz hung onto the wheel, all the boys trimmed simultaneously, and we exploded down the face of a monster wave. From my viewpoint, 100 feet above the water, it felt like we were flying, literally." Jerry grinned at the recollection. "Anyone looking for reasons to do the Whitbread, this is one of them. Chasing fronts and sailing on the edge make this a race without equal."

On Day 29, *Chessie* had a brush with disaster. The topmast backstay shackle broke. The whole rig, with a large masthead spinna-

"There is no other feeling in the world like hurtling along at 20–25 knots of boat speed into inky blackness. The only light we can see is the five instrument readouts, like alien eyes glowing red, which hang from the back of our mast. This image would fit comfortably into any George Lucas film," wrote Fuzz. "Those readouts are our lifeline to reality when sailing with no horizon on these pitch-black nights. Since at times we are bundled head to toe, including goggles and our high-collared foulies, it's hard to feel the wind, and the readouts are our only reference. We might as well be blindfolded behind the wheel of a runaway truck. The helmsman and trimmer are sailing by the seat of their pants alone."

ker, rested on the safety strop [backup line] in 25 knots of wind. As the safety strop started to let go, the crew turned the boat downwind, unloaded the rig, and fixed the problem. The thin, 18-millimeter, Vectran backup rope had held and prevented a dismasting. Nerves, too, had frayed a bit. As Fuzz wrote, "We are having a very fast finish to this leg, but we have to keep *Chessie* in one piece to hold our position. Our fuel problem has diminished substantially. It looks like we will make it without rationing food or fuel."

America's Challenge had troubles of their own. Campbell Field, one of *Chessie*'s original crew, lost part of his finger during a sail change. The onboard medics closed it up as well as possible and carried him to bed. He had passed out. Campbell would have to wait until Cape Town for proper medical treatment.

As the skeds (position reports) showed

Chessie closing in on Cape Town, Jono's excitement rose. He was going home. "During the afternoon watch, I kept scanning the horizon for the first glimpse of Table Mountain. I knew that, being 3,500 feet above sea level, it was visible from a long way off. Success! I saw it from about 65 miles out. At first, a few of the guys said there was no way it could be land, but as we surfed the long South Atlantic swells closer and closer, it became evident. Unfortunately, it would be dark by the time we finished; at this stage, no one seemed too upset." As *Chessie* neared her destination, Mark reminded the guys that it had been 32 days since they had eaten fresh food of any kind, let alone drunk alcohol, and that the effects on their stomachs could be severe.

At 9:12 P.M. on October 23, *Chessie* arrived in Cape Town, South Africa—7,350 nautical miles and 32 days, 6 hours, and 12

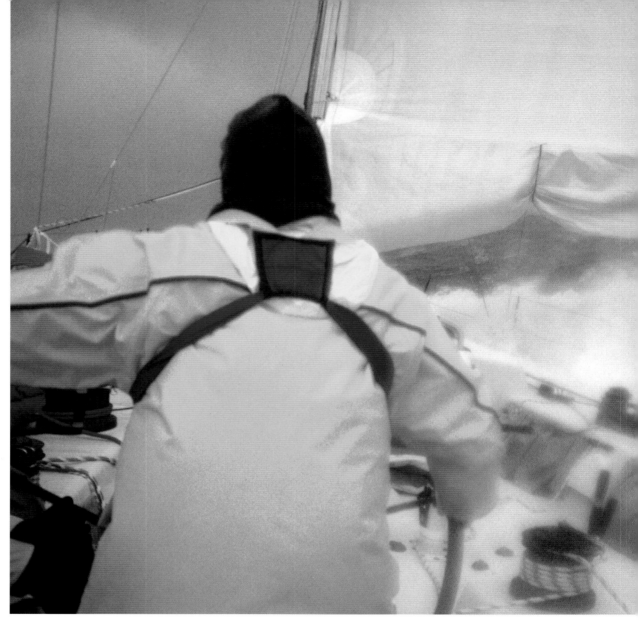

"We were flying along at 25.5 knots of boat speed. The only reason it wasn't more was because the masthead kite was pushing the bow down so hard that the bow wave was flying up as high as the first spreaders. The water coming across the deck was as deep as the top of the boom on occasions, and Talpi, who was trimming the spinnaker about halfway back in the cockpit, was regularly completely submerged," wrote Fuzz about *Chessie* heading down the biggest wave thus far, easily a 35 footer.

minutes from Southampton. The last few miles were torture. "After about a half-hour of no breeze in the lee [shadow] of Table Mountain, we reached across the finish line under jib-top and full main. As it was my home country, I was designated driver for the finish; and we finished to the cheers of our supporters in some spectator boats. Soon after, George jumped aboard, gave Rick a picture of his new daughter, and congratulated all of us. After one of the Whitbread officials inspected *Chessie,* we motored into the harbor and docked to the tune of our unofficial theme song, *Tubthumper* (I Get Knocked Down, but I Get Up Again)," said Jono. Everyone started dancing. "It was great to see the boys in such good spirits, with giant grins on their faces," Kerry reported to the Living Classrooms website. *Chessie* had come in fifth place, beating Chris Dickson (*Toshiba*) and Ross Fields (*America's Challenge*), the other two American boats.

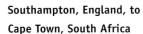

Jono's entire family lined the docks to greet him. While they fussed about him, he gave them a quick synopsis of his journey. "My personal highlights were having a whale surf alongside us at 25 knots, seeing the Southern Cross again, seeing the first of many huge albatrosses swoop around the boat, seeing Table Mountain again, greeting you and my wife, Cary, at the dock, and tasting that cold beer (Castle Lager) again!"

The crew jumped off the boat, sprayed some champagne around, talked to reporters, and headed for the *Chessie* "Welcome In" party. Most of the wives and children were there, but Rick would have to wait until Fremantle to see his family. With photo in hand, he headed for the phone.

FINISH POSITIONS AT CAPE TOWN

BOAT	OVERALL STANDING	LEG
EF Language	125	
Merit Cup	110	
Innovation Kvaerner	97	
Silk Cut	84	
Chessie Racing	72	1
Toshiba	60	
America's Challenge	48	
Swedish Match	36	
EF Education	24	
Brunel Sunergy	12	

Cape Town, South Africa, to Fremantle, Australia

LEG 2

DISTANCE
4,600 nautical miles

START DATE
November 8, 1997

ESTIMATED ARRIVAL DATE
November 24, 1997

Cape Town is a city of "haves" and "have nots"—extravagant homes built on the sides of cliffs with personal elevators to the water's edge and cardboard box homes under freeways. "This collision of cultures can create surreal experiences," wrote Steve Pizzo, reporter for Quokka Sports. "As I walked back to my hotel on a warm, muggy midnight, I could hear men singing. As I approached, I found a group of maybe 10 men, appearing quite poor, lined up singing tribal songs in front of an enormous BMW dealership window. As they sang and swayed, the sight of shiny, new, expensive BMWs behind them left me wondering how many generations would have to pass before the gap between the two images narrowed, let alone closed."

Finally, the crews had arrived in port. Being on shore meant crew declarations, boat and sail repairs, adjustments, and strategy reevaluations. There was no time to dally; the crews had to prepare for Leg 2.

According to Sonia Mayes, one of the Whitbread judges, "It is common practice in offshore races for the sailing instructions to require that a crew declaration be completed by each competing boat, stating that the boat and crew had complied with all the rules of the regatta during the race or the leg of a race. During the last Whitbread, a boat's declaration consisted of the skipper and each crew member signing his or her name on the same form, which was then handed in to the Race Committee within a set period of time."

Before the race this year's skippers had requested a new system to eliminate the gossip and finger pointing of prior years. The 1997–98 Race Rules required each person on board for the leg to sign an individual form stating that to his or her knowledge the boat and the crew had not infringed on any of the rules governing the race. The form had to be signed in the presence of one or more designated people within 24 hours of finishing each leg. "The new system," explained Mayes, "allowed each person to 'confess' in private anything which that person believed may have occurred on the boat which may or may not have been outside the rules. This system allowed each person time to think quietly of everything that might need to be recorded and reinforced the seriousness of an individual signing something that might be refuted at a later date. The repercussions for the current breed of high-profile competitors in this race, should this happen as a result of further action under the International Sailing Federation Racing Rules, could in some cases mean an end to a promising career or at the very least affect sponsorship for future events."

The Notice of Race and Standards Sailing Instructions required the recording, in the boat's log and on the declaration, of occurrences like the replacement of a sail during a leg, missing sail stickers, broken seals, the replenishing of supplies, medical assistance,

and emergency actions. Declarations normally took approximately half an hour. When issues or questions arose, depending on the seriousness, declarations could last longer.

During Leg 1, Campbell Field (*America's Challenge*) had lost the tip of his index finger from just below the nail, chopped off during a sail change. Being in a foreign country without a team doctor and having trained with *Chessie*, Campbell headed directly to the *Chessie* compound to have Dr. Rudi examine and restitch his finger. The onboard medics had done well, but the finger needed more time to heal. Much relieved, Campbell joined his own crew for the welcoming festivities.

Shortly after arriving in port, rumors began to trickle in. *America's Challenge* was in trouble. A middleman had disappeared with the syndicate's funding. At the ensuing press conference, a distraught Ross Fields, skipper, confirmed that *America's Challenge* was pulling out of the Whitbread. The Whitbreaders empathized; the situation reinforced the fragility of the sport. A somber mood swept over the Race Village as people realized the Whitbread was down to nine boats.

A day later, the second bomb dropped. *Toshiba* announced a crew change. Paul Standbridge, a Whitbread veteran and current member of the crew, would replace Chris Dickson, who was considered one of the most accomplished sailors in the world but was acknowledged as a very competitive, aggressive, and difficult skipper. Odds makers and sailing analysts considered the crew change a blow to *Toshiba*'s chances; her crew disagreed.

Despite the shock waves running through the Race Village, Bryan Fishback organized Chessie's troops. *Chessie* was hauled out of the water; work began in earnest. Replacing clips and shackles, lubricating nuts and bolts, going over the electronics, sanding the

CHESSIE'S SAILS AND THE WHOMPER

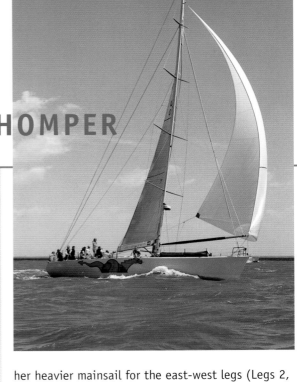

The whomper changed the complexion of the race.

Race rules allowed each boat 17 sails per leg and a total inventory of 38 sails, consisting of mainsails (the sail hoisted on the mast), jibs (small forward sails attached to the standing rigging running from the bow to the mast), genoas (large jibs that extend beyond the mast), headsails (smaller, inner jibs attached between the bow and mast), and spinnakers. As Dave explained, "The W60 rules prohibited large variations in sail rig plans over all the boats. Consequently, sail size was the predominate factor. We had 20 sails at the start, but quickly realized we would need a few specialty sails and a heavier inventory at the small end for the Southern Ocean, where the waves are bigger and the winds—always blowing from west to east—are much heavier. The entire inventory weighed about one ton, which we had to move during maneuvers. As time went on and *Chessie* was pushed harder, we built our sails stronger."

The crew referred to *Chessie*'s sails by numbers, which made sail change orders quick and efficient. The sails ranged in size from 300 square meters to 82 square meters. The larger the number or code the smaller or heavier the sail. The jibs were #1 (light-air jib), #2 (medium-air jib), #3 (blade; heavy-air jib), #4 (modified storm jib), and #5 (storm jib). The spinnakers, Code 0 (whomper) through Code 8, with their large sail area, kicked up the speed for downwind sailing. *Chessie* carried four masthead spinnakers (used in up to 32 knots of wind), one intermediate spinnaker, and two fractional spinnakers (used in winds over 32 knots).

Considered the accelerator on a sailboat, the sails remained a closely guarded secret among the crews. Long after the race, Dave reluctantly admitted that the mainsails weighed "around 80 kilograms" (about 176 pounds), with about 9 kilograms (about 20 pounds) difference between them. *Chessie*'s mainsails were made of 3DL, a three-dimensional laminate made with continuous fibers over a three-dimensional mold, which eliminated the need for seams, thus improving their efficiency in wet conditions. Dave chose the lighter mainsail for the north-south legs (Legs 1, 6, 7, and 9) and

her heavier mainsail for the east-west legs (Legs 2, 3, 4, 5, and 8). Because of weight considerations, the boats gambled by taking only one mainsail and hoping that it would survive without incident. Luck was not always with them.

The Code 0, the whomper (nicknamed such because of the noise it made flapping in the breeze), became a new addition to the Whitbread sail inventory. "Made from Kevlar, it was so large it had to be rolled rather than folded," explained Dave. "Other spinnakers were made from nylon and polyester, depending on their use." Lawrie Smith (*Silk Cut*), the original skipper for *EF Language,* started testing the sail. Cayard, who replaced Smith, continued developing it. The entire fleet had initiated development of the Code 0 and found it to be the fastest sail between 8 and 15 knots and with a true wind angle of 37 to 75 degrees in flat seas. The syndicates tried getting the sail approved, but the rules prohibited (1) genoas beyond a certain size, (2) spinnakers that could be used to reach or beat (points of sail), and (3) sails that flap. The whomper failed in all three categories; race officials disallowed the sail to be measured as a genoa well before the race. Except for EF, the fleet stopped developing the whomper and concentrated on other sails. That decision cost them heavily. Cayard continued developing the sail and found a way to get the whomper measured as a spinnaker despite its use.

bottom, checking for nicks and scrapes, mending and replacing sails with heavier ones—it was a team effort. In addition, the crew made some improvements to the boat. Leg 1 had given them an opportunity to determine what worked and what needed changing.

One critical improvement was developing a Code 0, better known as the whomper. With a sail area of 200 square meters, the whomper was a huge, unwieldy sail that combined the shape of a genoa (a large jib that extends beyond the mast) with the area of a spinnaker. Jim Allsopp explained: "Before the start of the race, we had worked on a similar design to be used for the middle ground between upwind and downwind sailing, but Race Organizers said the sail was probably illegal. Cayard (*EF Language*) found a way to get it measured, and it paid tremendous dividends."* EF had the new sail measured as a spinnaker, and it proved to be their secret weapon. Despite the protests filed against use of the sail, Dave and Stu had e-mailed North Sails to begin developing one for *Chessie* and were told it could not be available until Leg 3. Still, if *Chessie* wanted to be competitive, she needed a whomper. The other teams had come to the same conclusion. The protests may or may not be successful, but it would take time for each team to develop and build a whomper, time that could not be wasted.

The introduction of the whomper inspired awe and trepidation. A sail that size would make the W60s fly, but it would severely test their stability and rigging. The EF boats had been developing the whomper for years, and EF had built their boats with the sail in mind. The rest of the fleet would have to make adjustments to the masts and rigs to accommodate the sails. They were not designed to handle that kind of load. Knowing

that the whomper sail would put a tremendous load on the rig, Dave Beiling, *Chessie*'s rigger, who had been used on a contractual basis, was hired to travel to each port. Knowledgeable and meticulous, his skills and experience put *Chessie* in very good hands. He was brought to Cape Town for two reasons—to prepare the rig for the Southern Ocean and to determine whether it could handle the whomper. Dave took the rig down, checked every nut and bolt, replaced the running rigging, and strengthened the mast in every way possible within the race restrictions.

Linda Jones had her own work list, with one item right at the top—fatten the crew back up. The combination of limited food and hard physical labor (burning more calories than were being taken in) caused the crews to lose weight on each leg. Getting to port a few days before the crew, Linda and her new assistant, Laura Spanhake, Fuzz's

Dave Beiling, shore crew rigger, was a New Englander. He traveled to every port to guarantee that *Chessie*'s mast could handle the whomper.

*Peter Baker, "Chessie Dresses for 'Sail Wars' in Leg 3," *Baltimore Sun,* December 14, 1997.

The shore crew took *Chessie*'s mast down so Dave Beiling could inspect it and make needed repairs.

Linda Jones (*far left*) and Laura Spanhake (*far right*) oversaw *Chessie*'s meals, the only time the crew and their families actually got together, and made mealtime a time to socialize and relax. Laura helped Linda with the cooking and shopping.

Cape of Good Hope, the
tip of Africa

wife, found *Chessie*'s cooking arrangements unworkable. They did some quick reconnoitering and found a catering company with a dining room, halfway between the team's apartments and the boat. With some negotiation, they convinced the chef to allow them to work with him in preparing the team's dinners to be served in the dining room. It was not the ideal arrangement, but it was the best that could be done on such short notice. At least they had the needed equipment, refrigeration, stoves and ovens, sinks, and counter area to prepare high-calorie meals for the team and their families.

That left lunches. Linda and Laura prepared sandwiches, salads, and other goodies in Linda's cozy, apartment-sized kitchen, which she shared with six other Chessians. After delivering the noon meals to the boat compound, Laura and Linda hit the grocery stores and butchers, becoming very popular with the merchants as they shopped daily for

40 people. Then they headed to the caterer's and started dinner.

The sailing team got two days off, which they spent with their family and friends—climbing Table Mountain, touring the wine country, visiting Cape of Good Hope by land, surfing, or just wandering around the city. The shore crew worked during stopovers and took time off after the boat left port.

As the restart neared, the anxiety level increased. The sailors were going into the Southern Ocean, that infamous stretch of ocean considered one of the most dangerous bodies of water in the world, where they would confront 40-foot waves, winds of more than 50 knots, and icebergs. Cape Town to Fremantle, 4,600 miles of some of the toughest sailing known, had been tackled by some of the sailors before but not by others. While the families tried to show strength and support, the crews psyched themselves up. "You

Demetrio "Dee" Smith, tactician for Leg 2 and skipper for Leg 5, hails from San Francisco, California. Dee started sailing on the international circuit in 1974, winning the World ½-Ton Cup in La Rochelle, France.

CREW FOR CHESSIE RACING

LEG

2

Mark Fischer, skipper

Juan Vila, navigator

Dee Smith, tactician

Grant "Fuzz" Spanhake, watch captain

Dave Scott, watch captain/sailmaker

Jerry Kirby, crew boss/bowman

Rick Deppe, bowman

Greg Gendell, bowman

Antonio "Talpi" Piris, trimmer/driver

Jonathan "Jono" Swain, trimmer/driver

Paul "Whirly" van Dyke, trimmer/driver

Stu Wilson, grinder/sailmaker

know you are going to be scared to death part of the time," said Jerry Kirby, "but that is why you go." Taking a racing boat like *Chessie* into the Southern Ocean and coming back intact would be a major accomplishment, but it allowed no room for error. The sailors were anxious to test themselves against Mother Nature in the Southern Ocean. Their families were anxious to have them return safely.

Over the years, the role of navigator had evolved. It now required knowledge of meteorology and strategy, while computers charted various possible courses. Based on weather patterns and fleet positions, the navigator and skipper would determine which course best suited their needs. Juan Vila pored over his charts and weather predictions. Between 40 and 60 degrees south latitude, the Southern Ocean remains one of the windiest and most desolate parts of the world. Because few people travel the area, weather forecasters pay the ocean comparatively scant attention. As a result, the sailors had to rely on thin, if not unreliable, data. Low pressures and high westerly winds are found farther south to a point past which depressions and icebergs are found. "How far south do we go, and when do we turn north for Australia? That's what will win or lose this leg," calculated Juan. During the regular prerace press conference, the other skippers confirmed his assessment. Standbridge, newly appointed skipper for *Toshiba*, grimly chuckled, "You get off an exit too early or too late, and you can have a big deficit."

Dee Smith, replacing Jim Allsopp as tactician for Leg 2, prepared for his first Southern Ocean crossing. "It would be great if we had breakaway speed, but I don't think any of the boats have that. The speed differential is in the sails and finding the right weather patterns," said Dee. "This leg is going to be won or lost leaving here, which will set us up for

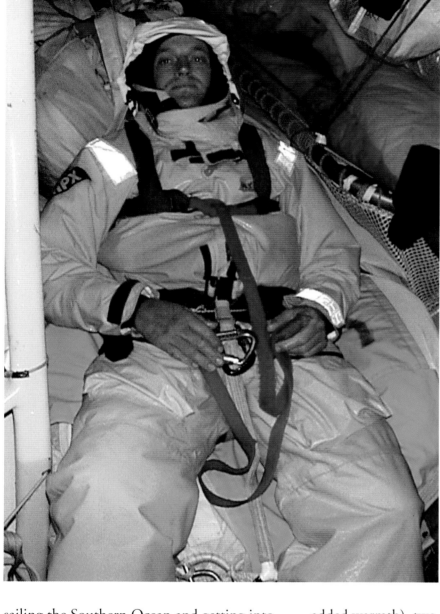

Rick took a moment to recuperate after getting dressed in full foul weather gear.

sailing the Southern Ocean and getting into Fremantle."*

With the repairs completed, the crew lowered the boat back into the water and then began packing. The expected duration of Leg 2 was 19 days—*Chessie* packed food for 22 days. Because of the crew's average weight loss (7 pounds) on Leg 1 and the harsh conditions expected during Leg 2, the team increased each sailor's rations from 3,000 to 4,000 calories per day. Packing for fewer days would afford the needed additional space, while crew energy output would increase substantially. The additional weight was deemed necessary.

The crew gear for Leg 2 would also be heavier. Each crew member took an extra pair of thermal underwear, a pair of fishnet-mesh long underwear (to create an air trap for

*Gilbert A. Lewthwaite, "Smith Named Co-skipper for *Chessie*'s Second Leg," *Baltimore Sun,* November 1, 1997.

added warmth), two pairs of Polartec socks, a Polartec fleece vest and pullover (designed by Open Air Wear), a heavy Goretex jacket and bib trousers (developed by Douglas Gill), sunglasses and antifog ski goggles (donated by Revo), a pair of boots, a neoprene Aquaclava and gloves, and, to finish the ensemble, a survival suit.

The survival suit, a neoprene coverall that protected the entire body, including the feet, was required by Race Headquarters. With rubber seals at the neck and wrists, the suit could be inflated with a pull cord if a crew member fell overboard, keeping a person dry and alive for about 3 hours. A few Chessians upgraded to a Shark suit, which was capable of keeping a person alive for 31 hours. Because of added weight, however, most of the crew opted for the lighter-weight survival suit. As a final precaution, each crew member also had an inflatable harness that clipped onto the boat.

Table Mountain's "table-cloth" began covering the mountain as *Chessie* pulled away from the dock.

The sailors dedicated the night before the restart to their families, heading for an early bedtime. "You can't go out drinking and then be awake a couple hours later to compete or train," explained Jono. "Until the end of the race, you are 'in training.'"*

Finally, it was race day, November 8. The shore crews scurried around the docks, loading gear and food, checking everything one last time, and having the sails checked and measured by race officials. The skippers and navigators checked in with the Race Committee one last time, and the families said their farewells. As the children cried and screamed for daddy, the spouses dug a little deeper for a show of strength and said their good-byes. *Chessie*'s guest slots were filled by George Collins and Gil Lewthwaite, *Baltimore Sun* reporter. With the South African

*Ellen Gammerman, "Executive-Turned-Sailor Readies His Crew to Race the Wind," *Baltimore Sun,* July 6, 1997.

Navy Band playing, the boats left the docks one by one and sailed out to the start line.

Instead of using a spectator boat, *Chessie*'s family members headed for Table Mountain and Lion's Head (two mountains overlooking the harbor) to watch the start. They then drove to Camp's Bay (a beach along the coast) to follow the fleet's progress down the South African coast and to enjoy a little beach time.

This was a bad start for *Chessie*. The wind was blowing at 10 knots, with lightly rolling seas. Under the shadow of Table Mountain, the breeze faded. *Merit Cup* limped across the start line, followed by *Brunel Sunergy, Swedish Match, Silk Cut, EF Education, EF Language, Toshiba, Innovation Kvaerner,* and, bringing up the rear, *Chessie Racing.* Boxed in by *Kvaerner,* Dee complained, "We've got our work cut out for us." Suddenly, he was shouting, "Get somebody up the stick; the top batten [a thin slat inserted in a sail to keep its shape] is caught up." Within seconds, Jerry Kirby had clipped his harness onto the halyard and rapidly climbed the mast to untangle the line.*

As the fleet rounded the markers and headed down the rocky coast of South Africa, as many as two hundred spectator boats formed a flotilla to see the racers off. "It was slow sailing along the coast," remembers Whirly. "*Swedish Match* made an early move that would pay off big for them. But it was early yet and there were 4,600 miles to go." The "move" was when *Swedish Match* sailed away from the fleet to catch a strong breeze blowing smoke from a freighter's smokestack. By the time the rest of the fleet decided to follow, *Swedish Match* had a very comfortable lead.

George Collins recalled transferring off *Chessie:* "We were almost on the rocks. It was only blowing 3–4 knots, which made it pretty scary. I was afraid we'd either be pushed into the rocks by the current, or the wind would stop altogether and we'd drift into them. It was not the ideal transfer spot, but our additional weight further slowed *Chessie* down." By the time George climbed onto the chase boat, conditions had changed and *Chessie's* chances were improving. "They're back in touch, in the middle of the pack; anything can happen now," smiled George.

By Day 3, *Chessie* had clawed its way into second place. "Made some good time last night, got into second," wrote Whirly in his personal log. "It's been light; we go well in light air. Things are tight in the fleet. Anticipating Southern Ocean cold, snow, 40–50 knots. We'll see what happens. We do need to get south to get the breeze. I'm overreacting, overanticipating the Southern Ocean." He was not alone.

The fleet approached the Roaring Forties

(Latitude 40), known for winds of more than 50 knots and waves over 40 feet tall. *Chessie's* crew e-mailed that "we get the feeling this area should be renamed the Whispering Forties. Here we are in the Southern Ocean, with enough warm clothing to mount a respectable Antarctic expedition, yet all we need at the moment are t-shirts and shorts." Was this another repercussion of El Niño?

During the next 24 hours, *Chessie* fell from second to eighth place. The wind had died down in *Chessie's* chosen course. The mood onboard became very quiet and somber. Joking and storytelling stopped. "We are trimming and driving as hard as we can to claw our way back from the depths of despair," e-mailed Dave.

In this desolate place, the crew's thoughts often returned to home. Whirly missed his son's second birthday; Dave celebrated his own birthday with an e-mail from his wife. Such things reminded the crew of just how

Paul van Dyke (*left*), better known as "Whirly," is a Connecticut native who grew up sailing. Here he is interviewed by Gary Jobson of ESPN (*right*). A serious competitor, Whirly's sailing résumé highlights numerous races, including a record-setting transatlantic run in 1994.

*Gilbert A. Lewthwaite, "*Chessie* Back in It after Poor Leg 2 Start," *Baltimore Sun,* November 9, 1997.

A different flock of spectators watched the fleet as it sailed down the coast of Africa.

much they and their families had given up to take part in this race—from birthdays and anniversaries to PTA meetings and multiple household chores. Everything fell to the shoulders of the spouse. Every so often a little guilt crept onto the boat.

As the wind picked up, smiles returned. Juan climbed on deck and informed the crew, "There is a front approaching." Dave recalled that, "to a man, those of us on deck started to smile; maybe the Southern Ocean would show us some of its stuff. As our 'brain trust' huddled behind the wheels discussing how best to set ourselves up in respect to the approaching cold front, thud, the helmsman ran solidly into a soft object below the surface." Rick quipped, "Wow, that felt just like hitting a dock." Had *Chessie* run into a large fish of some kind? Had her hull or keel been damaged? The crew began to monitor its progress more carefully.

Chessie had been racing side by side with *EF Language* and *Silk Cut* for days. Now *Chessie* was losing ground. The crew peered down their endoscope, a mechanism used to view the keel and rudder for seaweed, plastic, or any foreign bodies. "The water down here is so clear that it is possible to watch the bow drive through the waves and the wake trailing out from the stern, along with the air bubbles that are produced by and move along the hull," wrote Dave. But they saw nothing that could slow down the boat. Still, it just didn't feel right to Mark. Jerry volunteered to go below and check the keel or rudder for damage. He donned layers of clothing, including two dry suits and some flippers, the crew dropped the sails, and Jerry dove into the freezing water. Unfortunately, the air pocket between the suits prevented him from submerging. After a couple of tries, he reluctantly opened the neck to allow the air out and the freezing water in. A few quick dives

Antonio Piris, trimmer/
driver/boatbuilder, goes
by the name "Talpi." He
has 10 boats to his
credit, including three
America's Cup boats and
three W60s. Talpi is a
superb driver. Active in
the world racing circuit,
this was his second
Whitbread.

showed him the problem—the front of the keel was slightly dented.

Shivering, Jerry climbed back on board. Juan met him with a bucket of warm fresh water to rinse the salt water from his hair and to warm his head while his teammates took care of the mask, fins, and safety line that Jerry had used. Jerry went below, peeled off his now wet clothes, and climbed into a sleeping bag to warm up. "Approximately four feet down from the hull and extending down four or five feet, the front of the keel was blunted and brown and the fairing compound had been crushed, leaving a ragged edge. A small crack had also opened up at the top of the keel where it meets the hull," he reported. That explained why *Chessie* had been running a bit off the pace. The crew surmised that the earlier "thud" had probably been a run-in with a whale. *Chessie* still had 3,200 miles to go. Unable to obtain maximum speed, the crew would have to rely on

tactics and patience to beat the Southern Ocean and the other boats.

With a wind speed of 30 knots and a boat speed of 18 knots, the crew's spirits rose. "Yahoo!" wrote Fuzz. "The Southern Ocean is here at last. It's just how I remember it—overcast skies, very cold, very wet, towering seas. Flying along finally with a reaching spinnaker set, everybody on watch is working his tail off to catch the next wave. We are approximately 70 miles south of the bulk of the fleet in an effort to stay in the low pressure longer. This scenario is finally starting to pay off." Then the Southern Ocean pounded them, and Mother Nature decided to teach them another lesson on respect. A major breakdown—the Code 5 spinnaker blew. Stu and Dave dragged the sail below deck and began piecing the bits back together.

"Ugly in the Southern Ocean. Anticipation is over," logged Whirly. "We had a good taste of it, but now I know I'll make it. We're

cooking along—cold, cold, cold. Tonight will be the coldest yet and the furthest south —hands and face are the worst. I still have some warmer stuff to put on. Speed 25 knots. Lots of spray—tomorrow we'll be heading back north, might not be so bad. Now it's cold, cold, cold. I'll be able to write more when it warms up."

Chessie chose to go south of Kerguelen Island, seeking more wind pressure. Kerguelen Island, a French territory, lies midway between Africa and Australia. Its average temperature is 1–2°C. The 50 to 100 people who live on the island are mainly geologists, geophysicists, meteorologists, oceanographers, ornithologists, and biologists. Kerguelen is located in an archipelago of 85 islands in what folklore labels the Screaming Fifties because it lies along Latitude 50 and the winds continuously howl through the islands. Winds in excess of 60 knots per hour

roar through the area at least 300 days a year, and winds exceed 90 knots per hour about 140 days a year. Typical wave heights measure 40–50 feet. The southern side is the wildest. The day *Chessie* sailed by the air temperature registered 1°C (33.8°F), and the water temperature was 3°C (37.4°F).

Chessie's "southern strategy" nonetheless paid dividends. "It was *Chessie Racing* that made the most aggressive move south," wrote Mark Chisnell, Whitbread reporter, "and she has been the biggest beneficiary of the reshuffle." *Chessie* had moved up to fifth. In an attempt to get warm, some of the crew blew up their survival suits for insulation. Although cold, they were happy and they were having the ride of a lifetime. Dave called it "Mr. Toad's Wild Ride." Ski goggles became a permanent fixture on the face. Without them, the crew would have been unable to trim the sails or read the instrument panels.

Racing on the Southern
Ocean

With two Whitbreads
under his belt, Fuzz
moaned, "'Don't ever
come down here again.'
Why didn't I read my
log. Stupid, stupid,
stupid."

Gunnar Krantz (*Swedish Match*) reported to Race Headquarters that "the face masks are on, and it covers the panic smile on the face of the helmsman going down the now very big waves. It is just amazing how much water comes across the deck. The closest to this is being towed by the feet behind a powerboat in 25 knots. Everybody is grinding, shouting, tailing, bailing water, pushing hard."

Repairs, difficult at best, could be life threatening in the Southern Ocean. *Chessie*'s boom vang (a block-and-tackle system that pulls the boom down to assist sail control) snapped. Talpi, a boatbuilder by trade, got to work immediately. Wipeouts were the source of many breakages. Mark Rudiger, *EF Language* navigator, tried to warn the crew of a serious-looking squall. "We went into a full-on spin out and lay on our side for what seemed like minutes," he recalled. Almost at the same time, *Chessie* blew up her Code 6

spinnaker and her staysail on just such a wipeout. While recovering, she lost eight miles to *Silk Cut*.

The pattern of this leg demonstrated again how the rich get richer. The leaders of the pack picked up the wind first and kept it longest, enjoying record-breaking speeds. *Swedish Match* was clocked at 31.5 knots. *Silk Cut* broke the world record for the fastest 24-hour run for a monohull, covering 449.1 nautical miles. When the *Chessie* boys read the fleet e-mails, they burst out in a "Yahoo!" and looked forward to experiencing like speeds.

The race was not over. As the leaders raced toward the finish line, they still had to negotiate the "Fremantle Doctor," the semistationary high pressure that positions itself off the west coast of Australia, often resulting in a parking lot. If timed just right, a boat could count on 20-knot winds. Entering at the wrong time could bring a boat to a virtual standstill.

The back of the fleet continued struggling. "A stack of sails washed over the side, taking the stanchions and guardwires with them," reported Guillou (*EF Education*). Eventually, without losing any gear, the girls winched everything back onboard. Dalton (*Merit Cup*) looked for a miracle to improve his position, and Bouscholte (*Brunel Sunergy*), reveled in finally dropping off the back of the low pressure and being able to average just over half the speed of the leader.

Finally *Chessie* was far enough north to reintroduce the crew to blue skies and sunshine. The mood should have improved, but anticipating a sixth-place finish dampened the crew's enthusiasm. The boat was very quiet. Sixth place in this leg would put them in seventh overall. "It's not exactly what we came here for," said Fuzz. "With 430 miles to go, we should finish within 48 hours. Our fuel, food, and cooking gas have all reached their limits. We should arrive with nothing to spare. That is a credit to Rick and Greg, who have planned this out to perfection."

Accepting the inevitability of a lackluster finish, the crew went into "delivery" mode and rotated their jobs, bowmen and grinders driving and the rest taking turns trimming, grinding, and working the bow. Talk changed from tactics to where to find the best steak, pizza, and beer in Fremantle. The 18 days on the Southern Ocean had been exhausting and thrilling and were nearly over. The boats crossed the line one by one—*Swedish Match, Innovation Kvaerner, Toshiba, Silk Cut, EF Language, Chessie Racing. Chessie* sailed into Fremantle on the back of a black rain squall just after dawn. The crowds were gone or still asleep, but the *Chessie* family was there to greet them. The last three boats, *Merit Cup, EF Education,* and *Brunel Sunergy,* were caught by the Fremantle Doctor and traveled the last 100 miles at 3 knots of slow, downwind velocity. Leg 2 was over.

The crew reflected on sailing the Southern Ocean. As Dee explained, "What I have always enjoyed about ocean racing is the sea itself. This leg gave us everything from snow to warm sun and 0 to 40+ knots of wind. We sailed a good race, safe, with very little broken gear other than five blown-up sails. I never felt we were not safe in any way. Maybe we could have pushed harder." Whirly noted: "Made it through my first go in the Southern Ocean relatively unscathed but definitely not as competitive as I would have liked."

Once *Chessie* was tied up, Rick jumped off the boat to kiss his wife and son and finally meet and hold his two-month-old daughter, Isabel, who had been born at the beginning of Leg 1. The crew gave them a moment alone before joining in to meet the latest member of the *Chessie* family. Linda and Laura prepared another welcome-in feast, and the onshore circus began anew.

FINISH POSITIONS AT FREMANTLE

BOAT	OVERALL STANDING
Swedish Match	161
Innovation Kvaerner	207
Toshiba	157
Silk Cut	168
EF Language	197
Chessie Racing	132
Merit Cup	158
EF Education	60
Brunel Sunergy	36

Fremantle to Sydney, Australia

LEG 3

DISTANCE
2,250 nautical miles

START DATE
December 13, 1997

ESTIMATED ARRIVAL DATE
December 22, 1997

Fremantle is a sailing town, and its citizens came out in force to welcome the Whitbread Round the World Race. The crews were treated like royalty. Schoolchildren and adults lined up to meet their heros and see the W60s, and merchants gave discounts to Whitbreaders. Port organizers threw a three-week extravaganza, complete with a street parade that quickly turned into a water-gun battle between the crews. Assuring a perfect stopover, the weather of western Australia was ideal for surfing, touring, and other outdoor activities.

In addition to rest, rejuvenation, and repairs, stopovers provided a time for catching up with families and friends. Numerous long-distance phone calls per stopover helped, but nothing could take the place of a family Thanksgiving. Linda and Laura tried to fill the void by putting together a holiday feast. Sitting around picnic tables overlooking the sea, the *Chessie* family probably resembled the original Pilgrims. The tables were filled with 66 pounds of turkey, 20 quarts of stuffing, 24 pounds of

mashed potatoes, 12 pounds of sweet potatoes, 12 pounds of green beans, quarts of
cranberry sauce, a gallon of gravy, salad, rolls
and butter, and apple pie for everyone. Filled
stomachs and *Chessie* camaraderie helped to
compensate for being away from home.

But it was not all fun and games for
Chessie Racing. There was much work to be
done. For starters, *Chessie*'s keel, which apparently had run into a whale in the Southern
Ocean, needed work. Jon Holstrom took
charge. "The dent was not uniform. In
some spots the damage was nothing more
than a grazing, while in others it went much
deeper." There were two ways to repair
it—metal primer or epoxy. Because of time
constraints, Jon chose the epoxy. Still,
the repair was not quick, involving a 10-step
process of sanding, painting, and filling the
minute holes with epoxy, followed by more
sanding and painting before a final wet-

sanding to guarantee that the keel had the
required perfectly smooth finish.

The team also decided to sand and repaint
Chessie's entire bottom by hand. As Jon explained it, "We could have used palm-top
sanders, which would have been easier, but it
would have taken longer. Time was not a
luxury *Chessie* could afford. Besides, we could
do a better job with sanding blocks because
you have more control when you do it by
hand. Everybody grunted up." The boat was
put up on scaffolding, and the team lined up
around her. With 15 to 20 guys working on
her, it took about four hours to complete the
task. "Elbow grease was needed; nothing is
free in boats," he quipped.

In Cape Town, the use of the whomper
had produced many a heated discussion. The
majority of the fleet thought that it should be
disallowed. The jury took a test sail on *EF
Language,* which some of the sailors felt was
useless, since a crew could easily sail the boat

Birthdays and holidays
were similar problems.
During the stopovers,
the *Chessie* family
celebrated belated crew
birthdays, but in
Fremantle it got lucky.
Stu Wilson was on shore
for his birthday. Armed
with whipped cream, the
Chessie kids gave him a
sweet, gooey hug.

Jon Holstrom examined
Chessie's keel.

a little lower to the wind (away from the wind) to eliminate unacceptable flapping. A protest was filed in Fremantle; it failed. The fleet would have to copy EF's whomper, a task the crews had already initiated. However, copying it proved harder than imagined. *EF Language* had had more time for design work; its whomper was far more advanced. *EF Education* benefited from *Language*'s whomper development. Before the race, EF had reinforced the top section of *Education*'s and *Language*'s masts to withstand the additional strain of the sail. As a result, EF's boats could sheet the sail tighter and use it in heavier winds. Race rules prohibited mast alterations or replacements during the race unless necessary to allay a proven safety hazard. Since the other boats could not strengthen their masts, the EF boats would be able to use the whomper to a greater extent. The inability to alter their masts, in

addition to limiting the whomper's use for the other boats, would require shore crews to repair and reinforce masts at every stopover.

At least *Chessie*'s whomper had arrived. Dave Bieling's constant attention would be needed, especially now, and the crew needed practice with the sail to discover its limitations. As in each port, *Chessie* received her routine maintenance—Chessians stripped winches, serviced engines and water makers, upgraded gear (a serious sewing machine was added), inspected sails, and made improvements. The crew also received its routine maintenance, real food and working out with a physical trainer.

All of the boats were being repaired and maintained, but the inevitable crew changes caused much speculation. As Andrew Preece, racing editor of *Yachting World,* explained: "With a Whitbread crew—perhaps more than any other sailing team—it is not the individual stars that make the difference, but the

FREMANTLE SAILING CLUB   FREMANTLE SAILING CLUB

CHESSIE RACING

MARINE TRAVELIFT
70 BFM

sum of the parts. In many cases, a team may have more success going with a group of sailors who are not individually the best at their particular discipline but who are able to pull together as a cohesive fighting unit." *Innovation Kvaerner* and *EF Education* made changes, but the big news items were new skippers. Finnish Olympic bronze medalist Roy Heiner replaced Hans Bouscholte on *Brunel Sunergy,* and George Collins replaced Mark Fischer on *Chessie Racing.*

Questioned at the obligatory skippers' press conference, George responded, "I can't wait to get on the boat and do a leg. I've sailed close to five thousand miles on this boat, but none of it was up against the Whitbread fleet. We need to get in the race, and right now. In seventh place, we're not in the race. So we have to do well in the next two legs in order to get back in the game. I hope I can bring us some focus." Kathy

Alexander, who had worked with George for several years, was confident. "I think the team will do very well on this next leg. George will be aboard doing what he has always done best—motivating people." Further energizing the crew, John Kostecki, Soling Olympic medalist and world-class tactician from San Diego, California, and Mike Toppa, a driver from Fort Lauderdale, Florida, joined the crew, replacing Dee and Whirly. Both John and Mike were well respected in the sailing community.

The prior legs made Leg 3 seem short (2,150 nautical miles) and easy, but the seasoned racer knew better. The Whitbread had added a stop, testing navigators and skippers while increasing the marketing potential of the race. The new route went from Fremantle to Sydney, Australia. Dave Scott chose a lighter sail inventory for Leg 3 because the only place he anticipated a good breeze was through the Bass Strait between mainland

In each port *Chessie* was hauled out of the water for repairs and sanding. After sailing more than 12,000 nautical miles, *Chessie*'s bottom was repainted in Fremantle. (*Chessie*'s bottom would also be repainted in Fort Lauderdale.)

Mike Toppa (*far right*), trimmer/driver, learned to sail when he was 11 years old and has participated in every facet of sailboat racing from grand prix level events to wooden boat classic regattas. He owns North Sails Florida in Fort Lauderdale.

CREW FOR CHESSIE RACING

LEG

3

George Collins, skipper

Juan Vila, navigator

John Kostecki, tactician

Grant "Fuzz" Spanhake, watch captain

Dave Scott, watch captain/sailmaker

Jerry Kirby, crew boss/bowman

Rick Deppe, bowman

Greg Gendell, bowman

Mike Toppa, driver

Antonio "Talpi" Piris, trimmer/driver

Jonathan "Jono" Swain, trimmer/driver

Stu Wilson, grinder/sailmaker

Australia and Tasmania, which is notorious for bad weather, big, tricky winds, and strong currents. "We'll be using our 3DL [three-dimensional laminate] main," explained Dave. "It's light but exceptionally strong. In addition, we will carry our new whomper, eight headsails, and seven spinnakers [the lightest a half-ounce per square foot, the heaviest three and a half ounces per square foot]."

December 13, 1997—restart day had arrived. As Dave explained, "Despite our lackluster showing in Leg 2, the *Chessie* camp is still very upbeat. It's hard to keep saying this, but we do keep learning. We know the boat has plenty of potential, and without a doubt, this is the leg in which we must perform."* As *Chessie* left the dock, George yelled, "Don't write us off yet! We're still in there fighting."

*Bruce Stannard, "Leg 3: Guarding against Runaway Winner," *Baltimore Sun*, December 10, 1997.

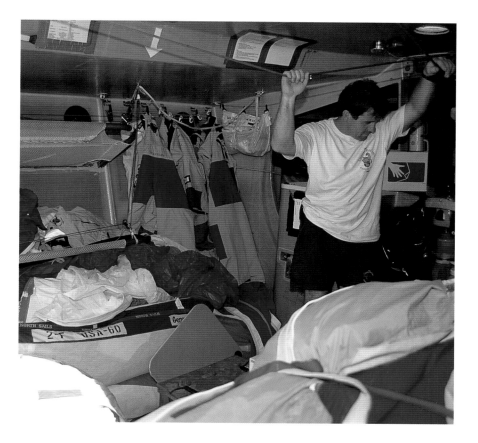

Below deck, sails, sails, and more sails were stacked everywhere. Personal gear was neatly tucked into unbelievably small bags. Foul weather gear and harnesses hung both port (left) and starboard (right). Large, heavy bags of food bedded down in the bunks. Space was at a premium because the front 15 feet and the back 8 feet of the boat were off-limits. What was left had to contain not only all the gear, but also a galley (a sink and two camp stoves that sufficed as a kitchen), a head (a bathroom with no door that consisted of a toilet without a seat), fuel and water tanks, 12 bunks, a media station, a navigator's station, and two engines. When heeling, all the gear had to be moved to the high side of the boat for additional ballast.

George (*left*) and John Kostecki (*middle*) talk to reporters. John, *Chessie*'s tactician for Legs 3, 4, and 7 and skipper for Legs 6, 8, and 9, is known as a cerebral sailor who can always see the big picture. He was named 1988 Rolex Yachtsman of the Year.

The fleet was closely matched.

Talpi Piris was similarly optimistic. "After improving our water skiing skills and surviving crazy western Australian physical trainers, we were all set for an intense 10-day sprint," he explained. JT (John Thackwray), a revered member of the shore crew, Gary Jobson of ESPN, and Kerry Fishback, writing for the Whitbread Education Project, were the guests for the start. With the sun shining, a good wind of 20 to 25 knots, hundreds of spectator boats nearby, a flock of helicopters overhead, and thousands of fans lining the shoreline, they were off.

Chessie led the fleet across the start line, but it was tight and the lead didn't last. A failed chute opening took away *Chessie*'s early glory. The lead changed hands three times in the first 15 minutes. After the first hour, the lineup was *EF Language, Swedish Match, Merit Cup, Toshiba, Chessie Racing, Silk Cut, Brunel Sunergy, EF Education,* and *Innovation Kvaerner.* As the boats headed north to

SATURDAY, DECEMBER 13, 1997.
ABOARD *CHESSIE RACING*, START REPORT
BY KERRY FISHBACK

12:00 NOON: *Chessie* and her crew pulled away from the dock. I've come onboard with two cameras and an extra lens, a notebook and pen, foul weather gear, a sweatshirt, and a waterproof bag (in case I am forced to disembark by launching myself and my belongings into the shark-infested waters off Fremantle instead of stepping gracefully into the awaiting chase boat). Since my husband is designated driver of the chase boat, I am secretly assured that I will not have to risk anything to the sharks. I set up shop and park myself on the two life rafts, which are mounted in the very back of the cockpit. Safe spot: behind all the action and almost completely free of anything that moves. (Although later I would be caught as the topmast backstay block snagged on the life raft and began lifting me and it off the deck.)

12:15 P.M.: A team meeting is always held on the way out to the starting line. George begins by reminding everyone to communicate. "Minds are like parachutes. They only function when open," he

said. John Kostecki, who joined *Chessie* as tactician for this leg, will be driving at the start. It will be a downwind start, probably a fetch [straight shot] to the first mark, which is five miles to the north along the beach. Spectator boats will make it crazy; we need to position ourselves in clean air [not blanketed by other boats].

We'll start with the spinnaker but must be ready with the jib.

12:30 P.M. (one hour before the start): The guys are planning to race this boat hard with all 12 crew on deck until 6:00 P.M. this evening, when they will settle into their watch system. Although just a blip on this 2,250-mile leg, the start dominates the meeting: sails, crew roles, approach to the start, other boats. In Southampton, *EF Language* won the start and then the leg. On Leg 2, *Swedish Match* set the pace in the beginning and sailed into Fremantle 19 hours ahead of the second-place *Innovation Kvaerner*.

12:43 P.M.: Word gets out that George has hidden away an extra pair of superwarm boots on board. The fine for bringing extra gear on board is $2,500. Everyone agrees George must pay $2,500 to EACH crew member. George later puts on his foul weather gear and discovers a candy bar in the pocket. It has become a tradition for the wives to hide treats all over the boat, without repercussions.

12:55 P.M.: Mike Toppa, who joined *Chessie* as a guest helmsman for this leg, would be calling tactics for the start. He and Juan go over their notes on the weather. The wind is at 220 degrees (southwest) and blowing 15 knots.

1:05 P.M.: Time is starting to stand still. I feel like I'm just about to launch the space shuttle. Juan and Mike note that the sea breeze is really starting to kick in; it's blowing 22 knots now. John watches the competition. George keeps time. There are 15 minutes until the first gun (it's a 10-minute starting sequence).

1:20 P.M.: The 10-minute gun sounds from the Australian naval vessel *Anzac,* and we sail by her stern through the puff of smoke. With 8.5 minutes to go, we are sailing upwind away from the start, timing our distance to get back. There are 10 helicopters in the air, with 3 of them hovering directly over us.

1:26 P.M.: George announces, "Four minutes to go." As if on cue, everyone goes silent. I can't tell if it's the buzzing concentration of the crew or my own anxiety that is making my ears ring.

1:28 P.M.: John shouts, "Two quick jibes now. Main in. It's time to start jiggin" [sailor jargon for "let's get going"]. We look in good position. Right in the middle of the line, with room on each side.

1:30 P.M.: BANG! Everyone was a little shy of the line. Our spinnaker isn't up yet—not good. *EF Language* hoists theirs, and they are off like a rocket. We started next to *Merit Cup,* but they also had a quick hoist and sailed away. Finally, the chute [spinnaker] is up, but the spinnaker pole's not right and the jib is still up. On one side, *EF Education, Silk Cut,* and *Innovation Kvaerner* are in a tight pack. *Toshiba, Brunel Sunergy,* and *Swedish Match* are on the other side. We break low for clean air and are in pretty good position, despite being a little slow out of the blocks.

Rick Deppe takes down the jib.

1:41 P.M.: Wind speed, 26.4 knots; boat speed, 11 knots. We are starting to get the squeeze as *Toshiba, Brunel,* and *Swedish Match* start to come up. John is doing a great job working the boat low and toward the mark, with Fuzz trimming the spinnaker. If we can keep this up, we won't have to jibe twice to round the mark. George changes spots with Talpi and starts grinding with Greg.

1:52 P.M.: I make the move from the safety of my seat on the life raft to the companionway [the stairs that lead down below]. It seemed like a good idea at the time. Good spot for pictures; I can see everyone's faces. That was until we had to take the spinnaker down at the mark.

We have to jibe. *Brunel* is just to leeward [where the wind is coming from]. Once we jibe to starboard, they're going to have to get out of the way. The chute is coming down. I can't see anything!

I'm stuck down below with Stu Wilson as he muscles down the spinnaker. Guess we've rounded because we're on our ear now [heeled over]. I can hear Fuzz on deck asking Stu to fill the water ballast tanks. Stu can't hear him. Stu, in his foul weather gear and obviously overheating, is moving all the sails up to the high side.

We are hard on the wind now, and I've stopped looking at my watch. *Toshiba* is right next to us. We seem to have good speed on her and make some crucial gains. The fleet is lined up. We are first in our line, followed by *Brunel Sunergy. Merit* seems to be a bit off the pace, and *Swedish Match* sails right by her to windward.

Going upwind into the waves, the boat has gotten much wetter. We are fully heeled over, and I decide I just have to make a move to the back of the boat again. I load up my pockets and zip my cameras safely into my jacket, check for waves, and head out. Much to my surprise, I get my feet planted firmly on the cockpit sole. I grope my way aft, and as soon as I get back on the rail, I'm told we are going to disembark up in the lee [shelter] of Rottnest Island.

Rottnest Island, only a half-mile separated *EF Language* and *Kvaerner.*

"The first night was horrendous," said Jerry Kirby, shaking his head. "We left with the Fremantle Doctor at full throttle and sailed into a pounding sea, with 40 knots of wind blowing directly on the nose. The constant abuse started to take its toll." *Chessie's* tack shackle on the headsail broke, and the boat dropped a place while it was fixed. The seas were so choppy that even this experienced crew suffered a bit of seasickness. "We must have gotten soft ashore with good food and regular sleep on a stable platform," moaned Fuzz. "We had long forgotten how uncomfortable *Chessie* could be sailing offshore upwind. At one point last night, I was lying down below sweating, as I was overheating in my wet weather gear. Feeling terrible, I hated *Chessie* and wished a helicopter would airlift me off this stupid boat that wouldn't stay still. The feeling soon passed as the next day unfolded," he smiled. *Chessie* had taken the lead.

With the boats still closely packed, less than eight miles separated the frontrunner from the last of the fleet. Suddenly, *Innovation Kvaerner* slowed and headed for shore. The rumors started immediately, via e-mail. *Brunel Sunergy* reported seeing *Kvaerner* taking jib and main down and preparing to rendezvous with a helicopter and hoped everyone was okay. The crew was fine; the mast wasn't. The emergency rendezvous, in accordance with race rules (a boat must be within a mile of shore to accept assistance), took longer than expected and required two attempts to complete. The first attempt failed when the helicopter ran low on fuel while waiting for *Kvaerner* to come close enough to shore. After refueling, the helicopter returned and dropped a repair kit to the waiting crew. Frostad (*Kvaerner*) e-mailed to the fans: "Yes-

terday night, in quite heavy seas upwind at around 25 to 30 knots, the outhaul hydraulic ram [attached to the bottom of the mast and used to tighten the mainsail] broke off the mast. A few hours after, Alby discovered that the whole mast was about to collapse in the bottom. It was buckled in the bottom on both sides. We are going to fight like hell to get back in the game as soon as the mast is reinforced." (*Chessie* had removed her hydraulic ram before the race to lessen her mast compressions.) *Chessie, Toshiba,* and *Swedish Match* all suffered similar but less severe mast problems and managed to jury-rig their masts. "We decided to keep racing, while praying our rig didn't collapse," Jerry chuckled.

During the upwind battle, *Chessie* was spitting water on the bows of *Merit Cup* and *Toshiba,* as the crew raced ahead before the beautiful coast of Australia. "It has been fairly rough, beating into rather small, short seas," wrote Cayard (*EF Language*). "We are tacking quite a bit, which is bad for the sleeping program, as everyone has to wake up and shift himself, sails, and cargo (food, spares, etc.) for each tack. We have been tacking on average every hour since rounding Cape Leeuwin." Van Bergeijk (*Brunel Sunergy*) groaned, "If designers make these boats any faster at these angles, we are all going to have to wear crash helmets inside."

Dave chuckled that, "as the boat pounded off some rather large waves in 30 knots of wind, the vertical motion of the body mass proved too great for the canvas structure we call a bed. Jerry and Mike found themselves together in the same lower bunk after one such mishap. Sleeping has been harder on some crew members than others, but sleeping at all in this pounding vessel is always an accomplishment." The crew had to take turns sleeping on the sails until Talpi had time to pull out the tool bag and repair the bunk.

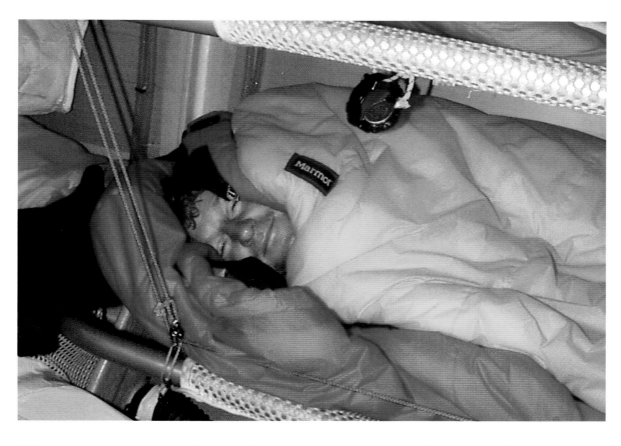

Despite the interruptions and rough seas,
Dave managed to get
some sleep.

"Toppa is a pretty heavy guy," grinned Talpi. The guys were resigned to the fact that they might have to sail all the way to the Bass Straits upwind. Not much fun for the crew, but *Chessie* loved sailing close-hauled (point of sail closest to the wind) against her competition.

As Talpi explained, "By the third day we were quite worn out, between lack of sleep and constant sail changes. Some of the masts were also suffering fatigue problems, including *Chessie*'s, but she was still in one piece and showing good speed. *Toshiba* was our reference for most of the leg. It seemed like we were attached by a two-mile bungee cord. We took the same route and led the fleet for several days." The fleet stretched across the Great Australian Bight, with *EF Language* the farthest north and *Innovation Kvaerner* gambling by going far south. Frostad (*Innovation Kvaerner*) reported that "we have limited options this time. We will be the first one

into lighter winds. It's hopefully an investment worth paying for early on and then to get some payback later on." Talpi continued, "Later, the crew suffered the stress of sailing with the whomper on its higher wind range, watching the top sections of the mast bending whenever the bloody leech [edge of sail] collapsed. Only Stu was not worried; I think he even enjoyed it."

Two days from the finish, Juan emerged from his nav station with great news. "*Toshiba* and *Chessie* should receive 40 knots. We will blast reach [point of sail with wind coming across the beam] our way to the Bass Strait, leaving everyone else in our wake. Unfortunately, weather is not a mathematical science, and Murphy's Law paid us a visit," Talpi frowned.

As Jerry reported, "The wind began to clock around behind us and, when it settled in, it was a 180-degree wind shift with about

"*Chessie* felt like she was doing the Baja 500!" chuckled Jerry.

28 knots in it. This wind speed should have been no problem, but the head sea made *Chessie* feel like she was doing the Baja 500! I was in my bunk, trying to sleep, but the motion of the boat made it impossible." One by one, the boats' e-mails complained about the rough seas. Standbridge (*Toshiba*) described the experience: "[BANG] . . . [CRASH] . . . [SHUDDER] . . . [WHAM] . . . [SLAM] . . . [SHAKE] . . . [SMASH] . . . [SWOOSH] . . . [GUSH] . . . [DRIP-DRIP-DRIP] . . . Repeat all again at 15-second intervals."

Chessie decided to go with a bigger sail when the breeze dropped off. In hindsight this was not a good decision. "A sail change in these conditions was an extremely dangerous procedure," explained Jerry. "Because of the high loads and extended usage encountered on a W60, sails are physically attached to the mast by the use of quick-release clips, or strops. These clips can be released from

the deck, but they must be physically attached by a bowman shortly after a sail has been hoisted."

Rick remembers the incident only too well: "As we entered the Bass Strait, the wind switched and a nasty sea built. At about 3:00 A.M., we put up the Code 4 spinnaker and sailed along pretty nervously as we watched the rig pumping around in the nasty, unrelenting, short chop. We hadn't put the chute on the strop, as we knew it was a case of 'when' something was going to break rather than 'if' something was going to break. After about 30 minutes, the halyard broke. It was almost a relief to be pulling the spinnaker out of the water rather than the mast," he said, shaking his head.

"The decision was then made to put up the smaller Code 5 spinnaker. It went up with no problem. The watch captain came to me and asked what I thought about stropping off

After being flung around, that was the last thing I wanted to do, but time didn't allow me to think about it. I let go and WHAM. I swung into the rig and hit the mainsail, bounced off that, and hit the spreaders in the chest. I think whoever was on the halyard decided to just get me down and smoked me to the deck. After saying I was fine, I passed out."

"I thought we'd lost him," said George. Everyone flew into action. "It was terrible hearing him cry for help without being able to quickly lower him," remembered Talpi. "If we had lowered him too fast, we would not have been able to control it, making the arc larger and wilder. Finally, we stopped the boat completely and got him down with a seriously bruised leg and in a state of shock. Jerry was called in for medic duty again, and Rick made an extraordinary effort to not only survive Jerry's medical treatments but remain active." Rick grimaced, "I spent 30 hours in the bunk before coming back on deck, but I doubt I was much help. I could only grind and had to stand on one leg."

Overleaf: From atop the mast

The decision to change the sail also cost *Chessie* the leg. She dropped from second to eighth on the next sked. Frustration didn't begin to explain the feeling. Once again, the crew was reminded that they were guests of the sea but that Mother Nature was in charge.

As *Chessie* continued through the Bass Straits, George was surprised by the number of porpoises he saw: "There were hundreds of them!" The mountainous islands in the background provided a beautiful setting for viewing the wildlife. That night Talpi recalled that "light winds made it hard to decide between a light staysail [a second, smaller "inner" jib] or the huge whomper as we slowly sailed through the oil platform fields of southern Australia." The last day was one of the best of

in such rough seas. I thought we could do it if we had a few extra guys on deck and found a smooth patch of water. An all-hands-on-deck call rang out. We waited nervously for about 10 minutes until our opportunity came. John was driving, which made me feel pretty good—he is an excellent driver. Everyone was in position and knew what to do. The trip up and strop off went fine, but on the way down, we hit a rough patch of water. It can be hard to stand on deck in this kind of sea, so you can imagine trying to hang on when you are 50 feet in the air," Rick explained. "I tried to hang on with all my strength, but it wasn't enough. I was flung around like a rag doll; I cannot describe the feeling other than to say I feel very lucky to be here today. All hell broke loose on deck. Flashlights were shining up at me. Somehow, I gathered myself and got untangled. Then came the really scary part—I had to let go.

After 2,250 nautical miles, *Chessie* streaked across the finish line only 53 seconds behind *Swedish Match*.

FINISH POSITIONS AT SYDNEY

BOAT	OVERALL STANDING
EF Language	302
Swedish Match	253
Chessie Racing	132
Merit Cup	228
Innovation Kvaerner	267
Toshiba	207
Silk Cut	208
Brunel Sunergy	66
EF Education	80

the whole race, according to Talpi. The coastline, helicopters, and tight sailing rejuvenated the crew. All it took was an extra effort to round one rocky point, and *Chessie* was off. Talpi recounted: "As the sun came up, we were in sight of the whole fleet, which was regrouping. After a few hours and some great tactical decisions from John and Juan, *Chessie* was making her way fast forward with Jono at the wheel. Mike, Dave, and Fuzz showed the fleet how a good Code 3 should be trimmed, while Stu, Greg, and Jerry supplied the horsepower." *Innovation Kvaerner, Merit Cup, Silk Cut,* and *Chessie* headed toward the shoreline in bright sunshine. *Chessie* overtook *Silk Cut.* Noting the breeze outside and gains from the boats behind and farther offshore, John turned to George and said, "I think we should go out. What do you think?" George agreed and *Chessie* took off. That strategic call moved *Chessie* ahead of *Kvaerner* and *Merit Cup* and set *Chessie* up for a podium finish.

December 23, 1997—
In time for Christmas,
the crew was in great
spirits and their sup-
porters were very proud.
Chessie had her first
podium finish.

"It was tight, it was dark, and we were
flying into Sydney with a podium finish for
our Christmas present," Talpi grinned. In the
closest finish in Whitbread history, *Chessie
Racing* crossed the finish line in third place,
only 53 seconds behind *Swedish Match,* who
was a mere 5 minutes and 8 seconds behind
EF Language. In fact, the first seven boats
finished within 30 minutes of each other. As
always, the sailors were greeted by the *Chessie*
family, including Tony Harmon, an Australian who had trained with the crew, and
Gavin Brady, who was competing in the
Sydney to Hobart Race.

Sydney, Australia, to Auckland, New Zealand

LEG 4

DISTANCE
1,270 nautical miles

START DATE
January 4, 1998

**ESTIMATED
ARRIVAL DATE**
January 9, 1998

With a third-place finish, *Chessie Racing* began to dispel the notion that the education boat, the "kids' boat," was only a sideshow. "We never said we were not a contender," George said in an interview with Bruce Stannard of the *Baltimore Sun* shortly after arriving in Sydney. "We said we had a long learning curve. How do you tell a 12-year-old kid that the boat he's rooting for is a losing boat? You don't. *Chessie* missed second place by a mere 53 seconds," noted George. *Chessie,* the education boat, the nonprofit, the underdog, had proven herself. Her crew had mounted the podium; she was a contender—and in the spotlight. "With John Kostecki on board," George pointed out, "we have a world-class tactician. Our confidence has increased, and we sail the boat better."

As soon as the dockside ceremonies were over, Dr. Rudi examined Rick, whose accident at the top of the mast had left him in bad shape. On crutches and with his cracked ribs bandaged, Rick would have to miss Leg 4, but Dr. Rudi was confident that physical therapy in Sydney and

George and Maureen
were chased by report-
ers.

Auckland would put Rick back in shape for
Leg 5.

Eventually, crew members broke away
from reporters and made their way to the
welcome-in party. High spirits reigned. The
crew had achieved its first podium finish and
now anticipated Christmas with their families. It was a well-deserved celebration.

The next day, the shore crew was hard at
work. "We had no doubt we could be competitive," said JP (Jon Patton), "and our
teamwork would keep *Chessie* going fast! We
were pumped!" With less than two weeks,
further shortened by two holidays, the crew
had little time in which to finish a lot of
work. John Kostecki had some suggestions
for improving *Chessie*'s speed, and, of course,
there were repairs to be done.

Despite the sudden notoriety, the crew
managed to celebrate the holidays with their
families. George and Maureen threw a
Christmas Eve party for the entire *Chessie*

family. Many individual families had set up
trees, of one sort or another, in their rooms,
and small presents, which had been packed in
Chessie's container months before, found
their way under the various trees. After a
fairly typical Christmas morning, the Chessie
family celebrated in Aussie fashion—at the
beach. Linda and Laura prepared a picnic
lunch. Cars and vans were loaded with surf-
boards, boogie boards, volleyballs, buckets,
and shovels. It was a day to kick back and
just have fun. Even Rick made it, but Dr.
Rudi kept a wary eye on him.

The next day everyone was back at the
compound, but a week later they were celebrating New Year's Eve in Sydney. The local
organizers threw a party in the old casino
building, and Sydney treated them to possibly the best fireworks display ever. "What
could be better than Christmas on the beach
and a front-row seat at a $2.2 million fire-
works display," said JP, grinning. Fireworks

were launched from skyscrapers, barges, and the "coat-hanger" bridge (nicknamed because of its looks). "Heads were spinning to keep up with the fireworks," chuckled Sally. "wow! What a show!"

January 1 found the crew gradually making its way to the container. Only three more days and so much to do. The alternating skipper system had started to take its toll. Each leg someone else, less familiar with the boat, was making decisions, which began to affect crew morale. To get the sailors refocused, George locked the sailing crew in the container for a team meeting. This was a critical turning point. With pencil and paper in hand, each crew member critiqued their performance and wrote down ideas to improve speed, communications, and overall performance. "We needed to improve our speed on the next two legs," George explained. "Our three-hour session had two

goals: to refocus and to improve team unity. Both were accomplished."

JP recalled that, "for such a big city, which never seemed to close, it was surprisingly difficult to get boat supplies, but evening entertainment was a different story." Although the casino and bars stayed open all the time, the Whitbreaders were becoming family now. Maybe it was the season or maybe the big city, but the crews sought one another's companionship more. With many crews housed in the downtown hotels near the docks, all sorts of unusual activities evolved. One night the crew tried mastering the didgeridoo (an Aborigine musical instrument), one evening was devoted to tasting exotic fruit, and another turned into a movie marathon where everyone tried to catch up on the movies they had missed over the previous year.

As the race loomed ahead, the crews prepared for Leg 4. Often compared to a game of chess on water, yacht racing requires as much strategy and preparation as it does skill. The Whitbread, because of its length and diverse course, demands even more preparation, with a dash of luck thrown in for good measure.

The next leg promised to be tricky. The winds in that part of the world could blow up fast, and the rocky coast of New Zealand could provide some interesting variables in navigation. Dennis Conner, himself, was taking the helm of *Toshiba,* coskippering with Paul Standbridge. George sent some of the guys ahead to Auckland to tour the New Zealand coast, currents, and harbor by helicopter. Juan Vila and John Kostecki needed to know what *Chessie* would encounter to plan their strategy. Local knowledge was also quite valuable, and *Chessie* acquired it by way of her three native New Zealanders on the crew—Stu Wilson, Fuzz Spanhake, and Gavin Brady. Her Kiwi transplants (all three had moved to the United States) were really looking forward to sailing into Auckland Harbor, their home and the sailing capital of the world. Gavin, considered one of the top match racers in the world, had just won the Sydney-Holbart Race. He was anxious to get some time behind the wheel of a W60. With Rick injured, Gavin would fill his slot for this leg. James Piper Bond, the president of the Living Classrooms Foundation, and George's two sons, Jack and George, filled the guest slots.

On January 4, under cloudy skies and with the Sydney Opera House in the background, the spectator fleet obediently lined the race course and the W60s maneuvered for position. The controlled obedience would be short-lived.

Sailing is a passion for New Zealanders; it is their national pastime, and the Whitbread is the World Series of sailing. All three of

Gavin Brady (driving), having grown up on a boat in New Zealand, is one of today's superstars in sailing. He is ranked second in the World Match Racing circuit.

Chessie's Kiwi transplants were fulfilling a lifelong dream. Leaving Sydney for Auckland onboard a Whitbread boat had been Stu Wilson's dream since he was 15 years old, when he went to Prince's Wharf in Auckland to see Peter Blake's yacht, *Ceramco NZ,* in the 1981–82 Whitbread. Exhibiting extreme symptoms of "Whitbread fever," Stu made sure that he was involved in every Whitbread from that point on, making sails or crewing. After training with the Spanish crewed yacht *Fortuna,* a highly modified and somewhat radical ketch (two-masted maxi boat), for more than two years before the start of the 1993–94 Whitbread, Stu's first Whitbread ended abruptly when *Fortuna* lost her mizzen mast and then her main mast during the first five days of the race. The Spanish sponsor pulled the plug. Rick Deppe and Whirly van Dyke, also members of that crew, shared his disappointment.

STOPOVERS

While the stopovers were necessary for boat and crew, they also proved frustrating because the time spent on shore broke the flow and concentration of the sailors. The Whitbread was in a league of its own. Most regattas took place in one location or possibly went from one port to another, lasting a few days or a few weeks. The Whitbread lasted nine months, stopping at nine ports.

At each port, the crew tried to carve out time for practice.

During the entire Whitbread, whether on land or sea, the crews lived and breathed the race. At sea, the crews pushed for more speed. On shore, they were caught in a holding pattern while having to readapt.

At each port, their stomachs had to readjust. After weeks of freeze-dried mush, the fats and spices of typical food, not to mention alcohol, could create havoc in the digestive track. Complicating the matter was the expectation that crews attend one party after another. Bland food was not part of the party fare. Instead, the local specialties took the spotlight.

The sailors' sleep patterns were also totally torn apart. At sea, their typical schedule was six hours

George and Maureen Collins.

on and six hours off during the day and four hours on and four hours off at night. Whatever sleep they got was constantly interrupted by sail changes and tacking. With each tack (turn), the sailors who were sleeping had to get up and move all the gear packed on one side of the boat to the other, including themselves. Once on shore, the crews were expected to work during the day and sleep at night. Then they would return to racing and have to switch back.

At sea, the priorities and demands were straightforward—safety and speed. On shore, priorities and demands placed on the crew were far more complex, coming from the crew and boat, sponsors, family and friends, press, organizers, and fans. The boat needed work. Sponsors wanted to be entertained. Family and friends came to various ports to spend time with and support their sailor. Children demanded attention. Organizers scheduled mandatory appearances. Reporters and photographers sought interviews and photos, and fans begged for autographs. The sailors were pushed and pulled and stretched to their limits. Their life, career, and sport required them to accommodate everyone. Somewhere in that mix, the sailors would try to find a few minutes alone, something they would never find when on the boat, and all the while, they were trying to figure out how to push the boat harder and faster.

Needless to say, the sailors could not wait to get back on the race course and get going again. And the shore crews were just as anxious to have the sailors back on the water. That would be the shore crews' only chance to relax and recuperate.

Each port had its own
set of mandatory appearances. The awards
ceremony was always on
the schedule.

After trying out with *Chessie,* Stu was
selected to sail on Leg 1 and secured a crew
position for the rest of the race. "More than
anything, I wanted to be onboard for the leg
to Auckland," recalled Stu. "I think that
helped me drive harder, pushing myself and
the team to ensure making the crew for this
leg specifically."

Stu considered the third-place finish in
Sydney, only seconds behind *Swedish Match,*
one of the best moments of his life—until he
stepped onboard *Chessie* for Leg 4. "Envisioning sailing up the Waitemata in front of my
fellow Kiwis, my family, and especially my
dad, I was thrilled when George gave me the
helm. As I motored *Chessie* down Sydney
Harbor to the start area, my heart was
pounding. It was being televised live, and
everyone would be watching. Please, God,
make it a good start," he prayed.

Gavin took the helm, with John calling
the tactics. Timing would be everything. As

the boats lined up on a starboard tack,
Conner, behind the wheel of *Toshiba* for the
first time, chose a port tack. *Chessie* had a
nice spot, just to leeward of *Toshiba.* The way
things were lining up, it looked like Conner
would force the other boats to turn and prevent them from taking *Chessie*'s wind, giving
her a nice lane and possibly a little advantage.
He must have decided to let the others go.
He was after *Chessie.* With 15 knots of wind,
Toshiba tacked at the last moment and cut
directly across *Chessie*'s bow to lead the pack.
Chessie was forced to pull up, but the maneuver backfired. *Toshiba* had crossed the line 10
seconds before the gun and had to return and
recross the line, this time at the back of the
fleet.

"We got a good start anyway, until we
started to unfurl our whomper," remembered
Stu. "It seemed that everyone, except *EF
Language,* was having trouble with their
whompers, especially *Chessie.* The tack fitting

Greg Gendell and Stu
Wilson hoisted the sails
while George monitored
the fleet.

CREW FOR CHESSIE RACING

LEG

4

George Collins, skipper

Juan Vila, navigator

John Kostecki, tactician

Grant "Fuzz" Spanhake, watch captain

Dave Scott, watch captain/sailmaker

Jerry Kirby, crew boss/bowman

Gavin Brady, driver

Greg Gendell, bowman

Antonio "Talpi" Piris, trimmer/driver

Jonathan "Jono" Swain, trimmer/driver

Paul "Whirly" van Dyke, trimmer/driver

Stu Wilson, grinder/sailmaker

[a piece of nautical hardware] sheared off, and we were left with the sail flogging wildly behind the mainsail. I had visions of the hardware catching in the mainsail, ripping it and ruining our chances for the leg." The spectators held their breath as Jerry Kirby wrestled the beast in. "After what seemed like an eternity, the bear of a sail came down," reported Kerry, onboard the chase boat, to the Living Classrooms website. "With all the crew scrambling on deck to get it in, there wasn't another sail ready to put up. It took another eternity to get a smaller jib up. *Chessie* was the only one flying a smaller sail, and her speed showed it." To compensate, John Kostecki ordered the boat to head up toward the wind, giving her a better angle for speed and a better position. Though on a tight reach when the crew hoisted her regular downwind spinnaker, *Chessie* was able to crack off from the wind and sail for the first mark, just inside the Heads (the entrance to

The tack fitting sheared off, leaving the whomper flailing.

After some tense moments, the crew wrestled the huge sail in.

the Sydney Harbor). By the mark, she was looking good, though still in eighth. *Toshiba* was bringing up the rear.

"With an excellent sail change and her tanks fully ballasted up," Kerry's report continued, "*Chessie* made an excellent rounding and headed up with speed for the next mark, just outside the Heads. *EF Education* and *Brunel Sunergy* didn't have quite the stellar rounding and were forced to tack to make the next mark. *Chessie* had already passed two boats. Heading east toward Auckland, *Chessie* locked into the 'groove' and began barreling down on her competition, overtaking *Merit Cup* before the boats were out of sight."

According to Fuzz, "the excitement of the start disappeared, and we got down to racing. After the mess was cleaned up, the crew looked up to see how much damage control we needed. To our surprise, we were still in the hunt. With such a short leg, it was im-

A school of porpoises swam alongside *Chessie*.

perative to lead or stay in contact with the fleet leaders."

As *Chessie* punched her way into the Tasman Sea, Juan monitored the weather forecast closely. Two days out and most of the way across the Tasman Sea, *Chessie* was in fifth place, running in 25 knots of wind, and still in contention.

"Gavin was steering in perfect harmony with the waves, gybing every three hours to take every advantage of the shifting breeze. On one of these gybes, we broke away from the fleet and gained 20 miles," remembered Fuzz. "It is unbelievable how a short gybe toward New Zealand can have such a dramatic effect on a yacht race."

Chessie's Kiwis were wearing big smiles as they approached New Zealand. Fuzz exclaimed, "It always makes me happy. As North Cape slowly came into view, blasting into the coast with a high-clewed reaching headsail with speeds in excess of 20 knots—baby—it is an exhilarating way to go home!"

E-mailing to students around the world, George reported that "the breeze picked up again last night, which is always a good thing on a sailboat. The best feature all night was one tack—only one! After what must have been over 400 times the night before, dragging all the sail bags full of water around with each tack, we were exhausted and beginning to look like big, overgrown muscle men. I think wet sail bags must weigh in at ten thousand pounds each.

"This morning," George continued excitedly, "we thought we saw three huge logs floating on top of the water only 25–30 meters from the boat. We were moving through the water at 14 knots at the time and were concerned about hitting something that big. All of a sudden, three water sprays burst through the air. The logs were whales, and they were lined up in a row facing us in U-

boat attack formation. Minutes later we saw another whale rushing to join the other three. They saluted and let us pass in review, like a parade."

Still watching the weather information very closely, Juan saw that there was a good chance the leaders would slow down at Cape Reanga, compressing the fleet. Could there be a replay of Leg 3? Fuzz remembered that "*EF Language* was hugging the coastline, reaching up Ninety Mile Beach and trying to cut us off at the pass. The cliffs at the top of North Island were spectacular, but there was no time for typical sightseeing." Still, George described the cape for the students following the race—high hills, a lighthouse, and mountains with sand in between. "How close should we go?" George asked Juan. "One-half mile," replied Juan. George had been warned about the big sand trap around the cape, the Columbia Sand Bar. Now Juan was telling

him to sail toward it. "It looked a little scary to me, but I have learned to trust Juan's judgment," said George. "He was right again."

Chessie had to find wind along this tricky coast. "We sent Gavin up the mast to look for it. What he found while at the top of the spar might explain why we had to ask mastmakers to fill in the grooves he left in his excitement," laughed Fuzz. "Three boats ahead—totally BECALMED. This could be our chance for another podium finish. What made it doubly exciting was to find *Merit Cup* becalmed as she tried to turn the corner to head south toward Auckland!" *Toshiba* was further offshore but closing the gap. *Swedish Match,* who had been comfortably in the lead, was stuck too far offshore. If *Chessie* could find enough wind and utilize it to the fullest, she could catch up and possibly overtake the front runners.

Gavin was sent to the top of the mast in search of wind.

Wet and tired, the crew was pumped.

"We felt for them; we have all been in that position once too often," explained Fuzz, "but *Chessie* was moving up. All hands on deck—no time to sleep—no time to eat. Even if we had time, the excitement wouldn't let you. Neck and neck with *Merit* and *Toshiba*—first, second, and third. We were within 100 yards of each other." Picking up the narrative excitedly, Stu continued, "We inched into second place. I was ecstatic. I was sailing home with a crew including two other Kiwis and on a boat I knew could win. I was living a dream," he exclaimed. "Moments later our Code 3 spinnaker blew. That was the end of my dreaming. As we sailed past my backyard, the place I learned to sail, I went below to repair the sail."

The wind died and filled in from offshore. The yachts formed a line along the coast as they raced toward Auckland. The weather forecast called for an increase in wind. In any

other part of the world, that would mean an increase of 5–10 knots; here it meant an increase of 20 knots. Despite the conditions, people started to come out in their tiny boats to cheer on the Whitbread fleet. "Only mad Kiwis go out in weather like that," grinned Stu. Next the planes and helicopters started circling. The wind continued to build. "We were pushing *Chessie* hard, Gavin at the helm and everybody in their key positions," he remembered. "It looked like we would be sailing into Auckland with a wind strength and angle *Chessie* loved. We still had a chance."

"*Chessie* was flying along in desperate need of her mainsail reefed to ease the pressure on the rig and maintain control," continued Fuzz. "We decided to wait until we got into the lee of Kawau, a beautiful island 22 miles from Auckland. The water would be flatter there. 'Holy #@*#*&^,' the wind had in-

creased to 35–40 knots. As soon as we reefed
the mainsail, the whole inside back end of
the boom reefing system came flying out of
the boom," explained Fuzz. Jono, one of
Chessie's best trimmer-drivers and her
onboard rigger, went to work fixing it. The
best he could do was a temporary fix. Would
it hold to the finish? "*EF Language* was
chomp, chomp, chomping away at our position, and we were running out of runway to
catch the others," remembered Fuzz. "Twelve
miles from the finish, I had just sat down
when the whole halyard winch fractured and
went flying off the deck and into the cabin,
where it pinned itself against the mast. 'Holy
#@(#*#^!' Drop the headsail. Rehoist on the
spare halyard. Chomp, chomp, chomp went
EF."

Back on shore, the support crews landed
at Auckland airport and were inundated
everywhere by fans (one of the hazards of
wearing team uniforms) asking for news
about the sailors. Auckland was electric, experiencing a terminal case of Whitbread
fever. "I was on my way to the Whitbread
Race Village to get on line and find out
where the boats were, when I stopped to
exchange money at a bank," recalled Cary.
"Tellers, secretaries, managers, and other
customers left their transactions midstream
to inquire about *Chessie* and the other boats.
I half expected the security guard to lock the
door behind me and close the bank until the
fans were satiated."

Given the brief sprint from Sydney, the
shore crews barely had time to set up camp
before the fleet was tearing down the coast.
Everyone scrambled to unload the containers
and get organized, but at the designated
update time, everything stopped as the shore
crews gathered around computers for fleet
updates. *Chessie* was a happy but tense camp.
She was again a contender.

"By now the breeze was up to 47 knots. A

Kurt Lowman, director
of communications and
team photographer, had
been a photographer
for United Press Inter-
national and National
Geographic before
joining the Blakeslee
Group in 1979.

freighter was trying to push us out of the
channel," remembered George. "Gavin was
at the wheel. You could see him calculating
our odds, and they weren't very good. I said,
'Gavin, focus on driving the boat and forget
the freighter.' He did, and the freighter reluctantly gave us room," smiled George.

Stu added, "Just off Takapuna Beach,
small boats continued to join the spectator
fleet and people crowded North Head and
Bastian Point to watch the finish. It looked
like we had third place. All we had to do was
finish."

As the fleet neared the finish line, the
support crews made their way to the docks.
Despite horribly choppy seas, the *Chessie*
family—including the Wilson, Spanhake, and
Brady clans—climbed aboard a power catamaran to welcome their sailors to shore
again. About five miles out, the seasick loved
ones spotted the closely packed dots coming

Gavin took the wheel on the low side of the boat for a better view.

out of the mist. It was a close race indeed. Kurt Lowman, our team photographer, was snapping pictures as fast as he could load the film. Fuzz's 70-year-old mother, beaming with pride, was trying hard to hold on; Stu's sister was giggling with excitement, and his father was bubbling over with pride. Rick, hobbling around the deck and trying to will his mates to victory, did a race commentary for the *Chessie* family as they screamed encouragement.

"One tack to the finish line, in 47 knots of wind, was no easy feat," said Fuzz. "The whole harbor was filled with boats of all sizes, braving the elements. The U.S. Coast Guard would have had kittens, but here it was the norm. People were everywhere." BANG! The gun went off at Orachi Wharf. *Merit Cup*'s main ripped as she crossed the finish line, but it was seconds too late for *Toshiba* and *Chessie. Toshiba* had second. *Chessie* had third. "Everything was starting to sink in,"

Family, friends, reporters, and fans demanded attention the minute the crews docked.

said a beaming Stu. "I could see my mum, dad, sister, and girlfriend onboard *Chessie*'s support boat. And there was the harbor I knew and loved so much. It was more than I had dreamed."

Fans swarmed the docks of Auckland Harbor, trying to see and touch the sailors. *Merit Cup,* with Grant Dalton and his Kiwi crew, was definitely the hometown favorite. Although painted yellow and white (*Merit*'s colors), the fans cheered for everyone, but doubly so for each and every Kiwi crew member. A few boos made their way through the crowd as Dennis Conner, the man Kiwis love to hate, was announced, but the mood was playfully teasing.

As *Chessie*'s crew mounted the stage for the medal presentation, Fuzz, Stu, and Gavin received an extra-warm welcome from their countrymen. They were home in their City of Sails.

During one of many interviews, George was asked to comment on lessons learned on Leg 4 and evaluate the crew's performance. George thought a moment and responded, "As for lessons learned, always go with local knowledge and always push the boat because it is an offshore event and things happen, strange things caused by fickle wind shifts. The locals learned how to sail in these waters. They knew where the sandbars and rocks hid; they knew where the currents and winds kicked in and how quickly they built. They even knew how to anticipate the fans' movements. These waters were second nature to them, which allows them to react instantly. Nonlocals had to study and evaluate the conditions before reacting.

"As for our performance, notwithstanding our mistakes, execution was much improved, but we still needed work for maneuvers to become effortless. We had good decision making, but it requires even faster execution.

Chessie received its
second third-place
award.

"*Chessie*, with another third-place finish, has made herself more competitive and a threat to the fleet," smiled George. "I would equate our performance to a rookie in the major leagues on a new franchise team, hitting 320, with 40 home runs and 120 runs batted in."

FINISH POSITIONS AT AUCKLAND

BOAT	OVERALL STANDINGS
Merit Cup	333
Toshiba	299
Chessie Racing	294
EF Language	372
Swedish Match	313
Silk Cut	258
Innovation Kvaerner	307
Brunel Sunergy	96
EF Education	100

From the top of *Chessie*'s mast, we see the fleet lined up in Auckland.

Auckland, New Zealand, to São Sebastião, Brazil

DISTANCE
6,670 nautical miles

START DATE
February 1, 1998

ESTIMATED
ARRIVAL DATE
February 23, 1998

LEG
5

After arriving in Auckland, some of the crew went out for some time on the town. "While we talked about coming across the Tasmanian Sea, we agreed there were some pretty hair-raising moments—but it would be nothing compared to what we would face in the Southern Ocean," said Gavin. The apprehension of facing the Southern Ocean revisited the crews—it was an ocean man was not meant to travel.

Leg 5 carried the most points of the race, 135 to the winner. It would take the fleet through the world's most treacherous seas, back into the Roaring Forties and Screaming Fifties (Latitudes 40 and 50) and past the infamous Cape Horn, the tip of South America and the graveyard of numerous ships. With only 114 points separating the top seven boats, "Leg 5 was really going to be a turning point for several of the boats," said Gary Jobson, ESPN commentator. *Chessie* was currently in sixth place, only 5 points behind *Toshiba* and 36 points in front of *Silk Cut*. The

With 100,000 people cheering, *Chessie*'s sailing team received the third-place award at the Auckland Awards Ceremony.

pressure would be on. As in Cape Town, the teams tried to avoid dwelling on the treacherous Southern Ocean.

New Zealand made that easy. With a three-week layover, the sailors got a few days' vacation. Some went north for more sailing; some went to South Island for touring Kiwi-style—bungee jumping, whitewater rafting, mountain climbing, hiking. And, of course, Auckland, the City of Sails, made sure the crews felt welcome. The Whitbreaders were sports heros and honored guests. But first came work.

After a well-deserved day of rest, the crews' schedules quickly filled up with Whitbread functions and parties, as well as repairs, debriefing, interviews, on-line chats with students, and practice sails. The shore side of the Whitbread was in full swing.

The awards ceremony was held at the Auckland Domain, a park overlooking the city, and combined with a symphony concert. An estimated 100,000 people blanketed the area to catch another glimpse of the Whitbread sailors and enjoy "The Symphony under the Stars." Dressed in team dress uniforms, the crews were instantly identifiable, especially Chessians in their *Chessie* green shirts. After each crew was acknowledged, the first-, second-, and third-place finishers paraded through the crowd to the podium. "With our unofficial theme song *Tubthumper* blasting, we made our way to the stage," remembered Stu. "The crowd was on its feet, clapping to the beat and cheering at the top of their lungs. We were sports heros in the City of Sails! It was a moment I will remember for the rest of my life." After the awards ceremony, the symphony put on a fantastic show, complete with a laser light show, fireworks, cannons, and dancing backhoes. Yes—dancing backhoes. To the music of Swan Lake, two pairs of 20,000-pound backhoes

performed what can only be described as a "sensuous dance" in perfect grace and harmony—only in New Zealand.

Dee Smith had returned as skipper for Leg 5, replacing George Collins, who again pulled himself for younger, stronger, more agile men. John would be off the boat for this leg because of previous commitments; Rick Deppe, being given the okay from Dr. Rudi, would be back onboard. Although some syndicates made crew adjustments for various legs, skipper and navigator changes made headlines. Vincent Geake, who had sailed with Lawrie Smith before, took over the roll of navigator for *Silk Cut*. Again, speculation and rumors swept through Race Village.

February 1—The crews had prepared in every way possible for their second crossing of the Southern Ocean and the rounding of the infamous Cape Horn. It was time again to face Mother Nature in all her fury. As

Kerry Fishback remembered, "It was a beautiful day in Auckland, sunny and quite warm but with very little wind. We had been swallowed up by a triple high-pressure system, which made for great beach weather but was a little tough on the sailing. The fleet had 6–8 knots at the start in a prevailing southwesterly breeze, making another downwind spinnaker start for the boats."

The fleet motored out to the start line. Gavin Brady knew these waters very well, and he shared his local sailing knowledge with Dee Smith. The spectators packed the shorelines, planes and helicopters peppered the sky, and every kind of floating vehicle imaginable lined the course. Over four thousand boats impatiently waited for the start gun and the ensuing turmoil. *Chessie*'s guests for this restart were George Collins, Charlie Barthold (editor-in-chief of *Yachting Magazine*), and Parker Rockefeller. Kathy

JUAN'S DIALOGUE WITH STUDENTS

This is a transcript of an on-line chat between students from North Chevy Chase Elementary School in Maryland and *Chessie Racing*'s navigator, Juan Vila, on January 14, 1998.

Juan, you are doing a great job of guiding *Chessie*. How were you chosen to be navigator?
I was navigator on boats in the two past Whitbreads. This is a race where experience is very important. Jim Allsopp used to race often in Spain, where I am from, and he is the one who first introduced me to the project.

When you finish a race leg, do you spend time eating and sleeping, or do you have to keep practicing your sailing skills?
The first thing I do is take a good rest. Also, it is good to have some normal meals after having eaten freeze-dried food on the leg. But then, after some days, you start preparing the navigation and looking at the weather for the next leg. This is an ongoing job.

Were you prepared for the high level of activity and ability that are expected of a Whitbread sailor?
Yes, we spend a lot of time doing physical training from one year before the start of the race. This is a race where the physical condition is very important. The more fit you are, the better your chances are to do well in the cold weather and the better the chances to do well when you are tired.

How is Richard Deppe feeling now? Will he be able to join the crew for Leg 5 to Brazil?
Rick did a good job in recovering from his injury. He worked out all the time during the past leg and during the stopover. And now he started training with us normally, so he will be okay for the next leg.

What kind of weather conditions require the most tacking maneuvers
When it is stormy and unstable, every cloud brings you a wind shift. In those conditions, you have to change a lot of sails and do some maneuvers like tacking and jibing to keep the boat going fast.

What have you been doing to prepare *Chessie* for Leg 5 to Brazil?
I have been looking at some climatology to find the average winds and currents. Then I look at the present weather over the whole course and see how it changes from day to day. I see how accurate the weather forecasts are that are supplied by our team meteorologist, Chris Bedford.

What is your most useful navigation tool?
The GPS (Global Positioning System) gives the accurate position of the boat all the time. All the computers are linked to the GPS. You can live without the computer, but not without the GPS.

Do you do anything special to keep yourself in a positive state of mind?
Just trying to know yourself and think ahead to the things that we can do better. If something goes wrong, we forget about it and try to improve from where we are.

What is your favorite freeze-dried meal? What is your least favorite one?
I personally like them all. I put a lot of Chesapeake Fire (a Maryland hot sauce) on all the meals. I prefer the meals that nobody else likes so I can get more! They all taste like hot sauce to me.

Do you carry a sextant on board?
Yes, we do. Having a sextant is required by the rules, although we never use it. It would only be used if we ran out of batteries or we had a major problem on board. In the boat, we have three GPSs.

What did you do to prepare for the weather conditions caused by Cyclone Susan?

Fortunately, Cyclone Susan did not affect us. There was a high-pressure wall between Susan and our course. As long as that wall did not get broken, we would not feel the effects of Susan.

Have you fallen asleep while doing your job? Standing or sitting?

Sometimes I have to sleep in the nav station for a short period, like 15 minutes, while waiting for the next weather fax or fleet position report. Every time I get five minutes, I use them to sleep.

What sort of wind conditions are necessary for using a spinnaker?

You use a spinnaker when the wind comes roughly from the stern of the boat. In that case, you are running. But you can also use a reacher spinnaker when the wind angle is more than 90 degrees from the bow, or between perpendicular and behind.

Have you met lots of new friends in the crews from other boats?

You meet all the other crews during every stopover. Some of them you already know from previous races, both the Whitbread and other races. You normally discuss with the other crews how the leg has gone, problems encountered, and so forth.

Has El Niño had an effect on the race yet?

Yes, El Niño changes the climatology, that means the average winds we can expect. You feel it in how strong the low-pressure systems are. They are stronger in the Pacific, and their path is farther north.

Thank you *hugely* for meeting with us today! We have one last question, but we want you to know we will all be keeping up with *Chessie* for the remainder of the race. We'll be there in

Baltimore! Question: Have you started to teach your little girl to sail yet?

She is still too young. She needs to learn how to walk first, and the next thing will be sailing! Thanks for having me join you today, and I'll see you in Baltimore.

Right: Chessie heads for
the start line.
Bottom: Fans jockeyed
for position to get
one final glimpse of the
W60s as they left Auck-
land Harbor.

Alexander and Kerry Fishback photographed
the start from chase boats; Kurt Lowman and
Maureen Collins photographed it from a
helicopter.

At 1400 local time—BANG! Instantly, what
had been total order turned into barely controlled chaos. "Just find a clear lane," yelled
Dee. *Toshiba* had her spinnaker set first, but
it was *Chessie,* with Gavin at the wheel, who
shot over the line first. As the boats took off
out of the Hauraki Gulf, *Chessie* led the fleet.
"Great job!" whooped George.

It was tight racing in light, shifting conditions. *Merit* and *Swedish Match,* with better
breeze, were trucking along the North Shore.
Closer to Rangitoto, *Silk Cut* was being
sucked up by the spectator fleet. *Chessie* was
bunched in the middle with the rest of the
fleet and thousands of spectator boats. JT in
the chase boat, taking the role of guard dog,
shadowed *Chessie* and waved spectator boats

away to protect *Chessie*'s precious breeze. The fans understood yacht racing and graciously cleared the way, wishing the crew good luck as they sailed by.

As the front boats neared the first turning mark, the wind died completely. *Merit* and *Swedish Match* almost stopped dead in their tracks. The boats from behind caught up with the leaders. It was a pileup, a restart without the gun. JT brought the chase boat

alongside *Chessie*, and the guests climbed off. "We had covered about six miles and seen enough action for a full day of racing," wrote Charlie Barthold for the Whitbread website. As the chase boat headed back to Auckland, *EF Language* finally put up her whomper sail and began rolling by everyone, but *Chessie* found more wind and crept back into the lead.

"Racing out of Auckland is always a big thing— lots of boats, lots of breeze, and thousands of people," explained Gavin. "Sailing is our national pastime, and we take it seriously down here." *Chessie* takes the lead.

Chessie, Brunel, and *Toshiba* stayed just ahead of the spectator fleet.

CREW FOR CHESSIE RACING

LEG

5

Dee Smith, skipper

Juan Vila, navigator

Grant "Fuzz" Spanhake, watch captain

Dave Scott, watch captain/sailmaker

Jerry Kirby, crew boss/bowman

Gavin Brady, driver

Rick Deppe, bowman

Greg Gendell, bowman

Antonio "Talpi" Piris, trimmer/driver

Jonathan "Jono" Swain, trimmer/driver

Paul "Whirly" van Dyke, trimmer/driver

Stu Wilson, grinder/sailmaker

The wind picked up. *Toshiba* and *Innovation Kvaerner* jibed for the second turning mark, sailing with a good angle and speed. With anchored boats unable to clear the course and the remaining spectator fleet racing to keep up with the W60s, the racers had their hands full. *Chessie* lost ground. Now in the back, she put up her whomper just as the wind died again. The new sea breeze was going head to head with the southwesterly, and the result was no wind at all. No one was moving an inch. From their spectator boat, the *Chessie* family members watched helplessly. "It takes a world of patience to sail in these conditions," observed Kerry. "The vast ocean can be frightening, but waiting for wind can make a sailor crazy." Rick was hoisted to the top of the mast to look for wind, and he found some. With him waving furiously, *Chessie* pulled back into the lead.

As Dee explained, "After three hours of sailing, we worked our way around and

Top: The wind died; the sails luffed.
Bottom: As the wind picked up, *Chessie*'s guests climbed into the waiting chase boat.

through everyone to gain a lead. On the first night, we opened it up to a four-mile lead. We raced the boat hard and stayed in front most of the way, matching shift for shift, headsail change for headsail change. *Chessie* was on fire!"

The winds died down for the next few days, and the crews readjusted to life at sea. Dalton (*Merit Cup*) reported that his crew had settled into a routine and readjusted to onboard eating and sleeping patterns. On February 3, the skeds showed eight of the boats fairly even, with only 40 nautical miles between them. *Brunel* had taken a more easterly route.

Then fleet speed changed as a front came in and the wind climbed to 30 knots. "One minute you are in the middle of a huge crowd, and the next you are alone," Gavin reflected. "I mean really alone, for three weeks. We had made it to the Southern

Ocean. No people, no lights, nothing but ocean everywhere you looked. I remember thinking, 'This must be what it is like to go into outer space.' It was so remote and so dark; I'd never seen darkness like that. And it was cold—really cold—bitterly cold. Luckily, we had good foul weather gear. Despite the cold and the darkness, it was the remoteness that got to me. I couldn't help wondering, 'Why are we here? We don't belong here.'"

The local animals seemed to wonder the same thing. Curious and a little apprehensive, the albatrosses flew right up to the boat but never over it. "Amazing creatures, the albatrosses are capable of flying in 50 knots of wind; they are the best sailors in the world," said Gavin. "In the Southern Ocean, you have to be in tune with yourself, your mates, your boat, and the environment. You have to trust your gut feelings." He recalled laying in his bunk, thinking about the possibility of

hitting a whale when, WHAM, they did. No damage was done. Still finding it hard to believe, Gavin chuckled, "It was really weird."

The first week went fine. During the second and third weeks, the yacht race turned into a struggle for survival. Whirly's log entry read: "2/6, 6:40 A.M.—Bit of a rough night. The Southern Ocean smacked us around a little bit. The outer cord [line] came out of the spinnaker sheet, making it impossible to trim [a combination of lines control the sails—without one, it is not possible to adjust the sails to the wind as needed], and we wiped out, busting two sails, some lines, and the pedestal handle. Lost 4–5 miles to the fleet. Glad I wasn't driving during the crash."

Chessie wasn't the only yacht experiencing trouble. When the breeze kicked in, the damage reports started piling up. *EF Education,* the girls' boat, suffered irreparable rig dam-

age. They managed to jury-rig it, but the girls would have to limp the three thousand miles to South America. "Yesterday the crew was completely demoralized by the rig problem," e-mailed navigator Beckley (*EF Education*). "Today, although still disappointed, everyone is back to normal and challenging for the speed record with storm jib and trisail [both small sails]. During the day it's crept up to 22 knots!" Their brother ship, *EF Language,* also suffered as they took the lead. Flying the kite through a 35- to 40-knot rain squall took its toll. "While reefing, Josh Belsky flew off the boom and poked one of the stanchions through the back of his calf. Juggy (Justin Clougher) and Klabbe (Klas Nylof) put nine staples in to hold it together," e-mailed navigator Rudiger (*EF Language*).

Whirly's log continued: "Twenty-four hours later, we wiped out again. This time I was driving; Gavin was calling tactics. Wow!

"Ice cold water continu-
ously came across the
deck in mounds of spray
as we surfed along at
20–25 knots," recalled
Jono.

What a night! The full fury of the mighty
Southern Ocean was let loose on us." The
lifelines were all under water. It was extremely cold and icy; the crew was unable to
walk on deck. "An all-hands-on-deck rang
out, and we were fighting to regain control of
Chessie," remembered Gavin. The crew
learned a valuable lesson about sailing the
Southern Ocean—know your own limits, as
the punishment is severe. Lots of things
started fracturing. "It got so bad you couldn't
name something that wasn't broken—sails
were in pieces, lines were tied together, the
radar was out, the generator died," Gavin
said, shaking his head. "The electrical system
shorted out, causing you to get a shock
whenever you touched the mast. The frac-
tures continued over the next two weeks.
One time when Jerry and I were on the
grinder—WHAM—in only 10 knots of wind,
the main winch just broke. It was so bad, it

was almost funny, and we actually started
laughing. What would break next? What else
could go wrong?"

Dee explained that "the problem now was
to manage sailing the boat fast and under
control while fixing all the gear. Sailing a
W60 in the Southern Ocean is all hands
anyway, but with one to three crew members
fixing things, we were left behind." With no
radar and the other boats reporting icebergs,
Chessie decided to take a safer course and sail
farther north. It cost her about two hundred
miles, but she still had two thousand miles to
catch up, which was longer than most legs.

Chessie's most serious, in fact critical,
problem was the broken donkey engine. The
boat's workhorse, it ran the ballast system
and the desalinator and charged the batteries.
It had been thoroughly checked in New
Zealand and should have been fine. It wasn't.
The amount of water shifted by the ballast

With the handles taped together, Dave took his turn at grinding.

There was no room for error in the Southern Ocean.

system was roughly equivalent to 28 additional crew sitting on the side of the boat. Without the ballast, *Chessie* could not sail her lines, resulting in less stability and less boat speed, approximately 2–3 knots less per hour. No desalinator meant not being able to make fresh water for drinking or reconstituting the freeze-dried food. Although each boat was required to carry a hand pump to desalinate water in an emergency, it required a lot of time and energy to produce very little water. To augment their hand pumping, the crew collected rainwater. As for the batteries, *Chessie* contacted Race Headquarters and got permission to use the main engine. Knowing they would need documentation for crew declarations, *Chessie's* cameraman took digital photos of everything that had broken. Still, the crew was in trouble. The race became secondary to survival.

Rick and Jerry, the onboard mechanics, got to work. First they e-mailed the shore crew, notifying them about numerous problems, especially the donkey engine. Next they tore apart the donkey engine and discovered the problem. Taking apart the head (toilet), they used some of its parts to get the donkey engine back up and running. Success—*Chessie* had water and a ballast system.

With that accomplished, the duo, with some help from Talpi, the onboard boat-builder, started repairing everything else, including the steering wheel, which had bent when Fuzz was washed into it by a rogue wave. "It took quite a bit to get Fuzz's shape out of it, but at least we could use it," re-called Talpi. "It would be replaced in Brazil."

The weather continued to worsen. *Brunel's* e-mail read, "Yesterday I was convinced I was mad. When I woke up in the early morning light to go on deck, I found a blast reaching boat [point of sail], throwing icy water all over me constantly. I had just gotten out of a soaked sleeping bag. Why are

Some of the sailors put their Gill spray jacket over their foul weather gear because the seals at the wrists and neck would act like a life jacket for a short time.

Icy water sprayed across the deck.

A WEEK'S MENU
FOR LEG 5

Onboard meals consisted of breakfast, lunch, dinner, and an evening snack. (Except for most of the evening snacks, everything required fresh water.) In addition to a Skandi Shake (a high-calorie energy drink), Gatorade, coffee, tea bags, and hot chocolate, the crew feasted on the following:

DAY 1: Cereal with dried fruit and nuts, spaghetti, shrimp Alfredo, Lurps (snack of nuts and dried fruit)

DAY 2: Granola with blueberries, beef rotini, rice and chicken, Pop Tarts

DAY 3: Oatmeal, beef Stroganoff, chicken rotelle, Gorp (snack of nuts, dried fruit, and chocolate), and peanut butter sachet (a 1½-ounce individual plastic bag of peanut butter, like ketchup comes in)

DAY 4: Cereal with dried fruit and nuts, lasagna, chicken Polynesian, high-calorie energy bar

DAY 5: Granola with blueberries, western-style tamale pie, chili mac, granola bar, and Lurps

DAY 6: Oatmeal, chicken teriyaki, chicken stew, Sierra Gorp, and peanut butter sachet

DAY 7: Cereal with dried fruit and nuts, sweet and sour pork, lasagna, raspberry crumble (requires fresh water)

(Note: Olive oil and Chesapeake Fire Hot Sauce were packed to help make the meals palatable.)

we doing this?" Onboard *Chessie,* Jono concurred: "The Southern Ocean soon humbles one. It was definitely some of the wettest sailing I have ever done."

With *Merit* recording its best run, Dalton warned of more wind approaching, "a VERY large depression is headed our way." Maintaining the highest average speed of the fleet, 19.4 knots, *Brunel* e-mailed a list of new repairs: "For the second time, we thought the rig suffered damage, but this time the safety stayed in place, and so we survived yet another squall of 38 knots. It sure takes a risk or two, once in a while, if we are to stay in the race."

As the front of the fleet neared Cape Horn, *Silk Cut* started to make her move but lost her mast instead, the culmination of a long list of problems. They had hit "something" solid that had dented the bow and rudder, creating a leak; hit ice that carved a six- by one-foot strip off the hull; lost the jockey pole (spinnaker pole), causing the spinnaker guys (used to secure lines) to keep breaking; broken a boom vang; and ripped the mainsail. Ushuaia, the first possible repair stop, was going to be a very busy unofficial port.

Bringing up the rear, 970 miles behind the pack, was *EF Education.* Its mast gave way again, and again, the girls made some temporary repairs and kept sailing. Refusing to allow their misfortune to ruin their determination and sense of humor, they earned the respect of everyone who followed the race. "Lisa and Katie have made an exclusive pack of [playing] cards out of sail repair material. This now opens up a huge range of possibilities," they e-mailed home.

The Southern Ocean took its toll on all the boats, and *Chessie's* own troubles continued. During a storm with 35 knots of wind, Greg Gendell was washed into the mast during a sail change. He wrote home: "After the

kite was up and filled, the boat took off to 20-some knots, right into the back of a wave. It was a big one with tons of water. I was clipped into the jackline and was thrown back to the mast in seconds. I bruised my bum and felt a bang on my shin. I got up and went back and worked the grinder to shake it off. When I got off a couple hours later, I went to bed. I got up after sleeping for two or three hours and felt my banged-up leg. 'I think I have a hole in my leg,' I said. I was feeling it through my woolies. I asked Whirly to pass me a light, and that was exactly what it was—a big gash to the bone through my shin muscles. The bleeding had slowed down. Jerry cleaned it and decided that stapling would be best. Eight stainless steel staples later, here I am. I am now on antibiotics and Jerry redresses the wound twice a day. It turns out I was dragged across the staysail's roller furling drum, which we leave tacked to its pad eye. It cut through my foulies, boot, and thermals. I am going to be fine, so please do not worry. Eight staples at sea in 40 knots in the Southern Ocean. Makes a good story, huh?"

"It was bleeding profusely," explained Jerry. "We were in the middle of the Southern Ocean, and we had a pretty big medical problem. I just told him, 'Don't worry; we'll fix it.' He declined a local anesthetic and told me to just get started. The wind was blowing really hard." With no lighting, Jerry relied on Stu to hold a flashlight. "The inside of the boat was moving so radically it was difficult to stand up, but to do so while stitching a guy's leg up, that's something else. I had three staples in when Stu was needed on deck. I stuck the flashlight in my mouth and finished the job."*

The Southern Ocean was brutal on the

*Gilbert A. Lewthwaite, "*Chessie* First-Aid Technician Gets Hands-on Leg 5 Lesson," *Baltimore Sun,* March 2, 1998.

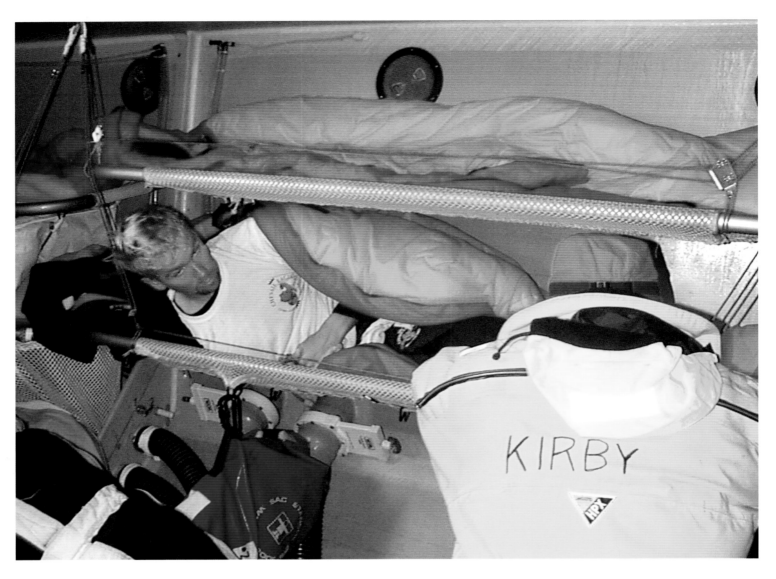

"Stitching someone up in a W60 is like stitching someone in the back of a Jeep driving full speed down a dirt road," said Jerry.

fleet. Lots of guys were getting banged and bruised by being thrown around by the white water coming over the bows. The sailors clipped into solid points like pad eyes to keep from getting blown back. "We are going to be the walking wounded coming into Brazil," sighed Greg.

The needed repairs kept mounting—broken head, broken wheel spokes, broken grinder (both handles had snapped off), broken stanchions, bent bow rail, and a badly torn main below the first reef. "Damage is increasing at a rapid rate, as we reach along in 40–45 knots of wind," e-mailed Fuzz. "Two nights ago, *Chessie* suffered a bad broach and the spinnaker sheets tore through the bottom of our mainsail. We had to put in a reef to save the sail. There seems to be little chance of repairing it before Cape Horn. The Southern Ocean is bad enough when we are at full strength, but now to be down here without a fully functioning boat is pure misery."

Greg wrote that, "for the past two days, the breeze has been in the mid 30s to 50 knots. It's great sailing, but we are all tired of being out here. You can bury the bow only so many times. The amount of water rolling over the boat is incredible. It gets old."

Still, *Chessie* refused to give up. Gavin Brady e-mailed *Chessie*'s fans: "When you think you are really in bad shape is when you have your biggest comebacks. We're coming back." Then the donkey engine quit again. No water, no ballast, and no spare parts this time—the crew was desperate. Jerry got on the ship-to-shore phone. "Jerry Kirby, Southern Ocean—We need some help. How do you fix this thing?" He tried every boat repairman he knew, calling Newport, Annapolis, the British Virgin Islands, Bermuda, Auckland. He was given a lot of suggestions to no avail; *Chessie*'s donkey engine needed a new starter. Juan charted a course for Ushuaia. The next call went to Kurt Lowman, operations central

A TALE OF ONE WEEK:
FLEET POSITIONS

BOAT	NAUTICAL MILES TO LEADER	BOAT	NAUTICAL MILES TO LEADER
FEBRUARY 12, 1998		**FEBRUARY 19, 1998**	
EF Language	0.0	EF Language	0.0
Swedish Match	25.0	Merit Cup	649.3
Merit Cup	86.3	Innovation Kvaerner	650.5
Toshiba	101.3	Toshiba	652.1
Innovation Kvaerner	108.0	Swedish Match	653.0
Chessie Racing	180.6	Brunel Sunergy	749.1
Brunel Sunergy	196.7	Chessie Racing	754.7
Silk Cut	507.6	Silk Cut	1,079.0
EF Education	1,077.3	EF Education	1,836.9

for *Chessie,* who in turn called JT in Annapolis.

JT recalled: "On Friday, February 13, at 5:07 P.M., I received a call from Kurt Lowman. *Chessie* had burned up her donkey engine's starter motor, solenoid, and wiring that lead to the panel. The first call I made was to the airlines. If I could get to Miami, South America would be no problem, but all flights to Miami were sold out due to Valentine's Day. After what seemed like an eternity, I was told one seat was available on February 14 at 8:15 P.M. to Miami out of Dulles."

Annapolis was JT's turf. He knew who to call and where to go. As an added bonus, Annapolis was *Chessie* territory, loaded with supporters ready to help, one of whom was able to provide helpful contacts in Ushuaia. "At 8:00 A.M. on Saturday," JT remembered, "I called Evan Evans and gave him a list of parts, and then I called the local Yanmar

Juan called Kurt to arrange the emergency rendezvous.

Rick tried everything to get the donkey engine back up and running.

dealer, the manufacturer of *Chessie*'s donkey engine. On his shop floor was a brand new Yanmar, the exact one onboard *Chessie*. Sometimes it's better to be lucky than good. Next, I called a friend who was working at the Miami Boat Show and asked him to track down two new grinder handles and deliver them to the Miami Airport for me. Luck was still with me. His booth was right next to Mack Boring, the company that had sold *Chessie* the donkey engine, and I checked the parts numbers to make sure I had the right ones. When I arrived at Evan's shop, all the parts were waiting for me. So far, so good.

"Around 9:30 A.M., I called Kathy and asked her to track down some charts for the tip of South America. We had to find a place for *Chessie*'s rendezvous. It had to be at least 14 feet deep and within a mile of shore. Finding the right charts would be hard, but on a weekend on short notice . . . "

Kathy called Maryland Nautical, one of *Chessie*'s supplier sponsors. Not only did they find the right charts, but they delivered them to her while she handled the curious reporters and anxious families and fans. It was obvious that *Chessie*'s troubles were making their way through the grapevine. With the charts and a few other needed supplies in hand, Kathy arranged to meet JT at Dulles Airport.

Back at sea, the crew was down to "three glasses of water a day and the sweets, as they do not need water," e-mailed Gavin. "I used to like chocolate, but three meals of it every day with no water to wash it down is getting to be a bit hard. As we all feel that we are getting weaker and emotions are getting higher, it is a real test of a crew to keep the *Chessie* spirit going and to keep working together like every other day." Fuzz continued: "The water that comes over the deck of this boat is amazing. Our bow pulpit is bent backward from the water pressure. We had to send Jerry to the hounds to change the snap shackle [a metal fitting at the end of a line] for a new one while trying to keep the bow from burying into the next wave, and I have my heart in my stomach every time there is a man up the mast."

The first boats had rounded the Cape. *EF Language* got around the corner before the wind died down. With the next four boats sailing at half her speed, she would be difficult to catch. Some very close and tactical sailing ensued between *Toshiba, Swedish Match, Merit Cup,* and *Innovation Kvaerner.*

The waiting onboard *Chessie* was almost unbearable. The winds had died down about three hundred miles from the Horn. Dee moaned, "We can take the problems with all the gear, but no wind is difficult." As they inched their way to help, they took down the mainsail so Stu and Dave could repair it. Still, the crew maintained its sense of humor and determination. "Rick Deppe, a/k/a engineer/McGuiver, has been seen scrounging the boat for parts to crank the starter motor," e-mailed Dave. "Last seen, he was chipping a hole in the forward bulkhead so that a device that includes a camera mount, one mainsail batten repair kit, various hose clamps, the ballast tank lever, and the donkey motor crank will pass through it to get some major leverage." Resourceful—but it didn't work. Filling the ballast tanks by hand took three hours from start to finish, but that didn't include making drinking water. Jerry Kirby compared the scene to a campfire: "At Camp *Chessie,* the campfire was a bucket, and the sticks for roasting marshmallows were hand pumps." When it rained, the crew saved the water for tea.

One hundred fifty miles from the cape, Gavin noticed more marine life as *Chessie* got closer to land. "The one animal that has been following us all the way is the albatross.

Evan Evans, electrician, moved to Annapolis when he was 11, started sailing two years later, and landed his first job in the marine industry the following year.

Watching these giant birds gliding along without flapping their wings for long periods of time is something I can do for hours on end," he smiled. While driving, Gavin saw a massive fin moving toward *Chessie* at twice her speed. "It was an orca. He had to be a big one because the fin was about three feet high," exclaimed Gavin. "He was able to turn and dive like a six-foot dolphin."

Whirly took his turn pumping water by hand. After four hours of hand pumping, the crew was lucky if it had accumulated two or three liters of water.

When the wind died down, the crew took the mainsail down to repair the gash.

Juan Vila, continuing to study the weather, noticed that the high pressure that had becalmed *Chessie* was now approaching the four musketeers (*Merit Cup, Innovation Kvaerner, Swedish Match,* and *Toshiba*). He informed Dee. "Maybe we could still get lucky," smiled Dee.

By now, JT had arrived in Miami and gathered the grinder handles; two hours later he was on his way to South America. "I arrived in Chile on Sunday morning," remembered JT, "and arranged for a taxi to take me to Ushuaia in Tierra del Fuego, since there was no other way to get there. A typical cab ride it wasn't. It took 14 hours and cost U.S.$1,200. When I finally arrived in Ushuaia, I called Kurt to see what he had arranged regarding a charter boat or helicopter. The weather in this part of the world can turn bad very quickly, so I was relieved to see a 110-foot power boat waiting at the dock for

me. Knowing the boys had gone without food and water for over four days, I went shopping for bottled water and some food (a few cooked chickens and some yogurt and fresh fruit) to tide them over while they fixed the donkey engine."

The rendezvous boat, loaded with the supplies, traveled 120 miles toward the cape. Some 14 hours later, they spotted *Chessie* drifting. The wind had died completely. With the rocky coast and the risk of the current pushing *Chessie* into the rocks, Dee read the rules yet again and gave the go-ahead for *Chessie* to be towed to the rendezvous spot. They anchored off Cabo Buen Suceso, at the eastern tip of Tierra del Fuego, Argentina. "Never has anyone been happier to see JT. He was the man," exclaimed Greg. "The transfer took exactly one hour and one minute, including towing. We hoisted the sails and were off," recalled Gavin. "Jerry and

The crew took the sails down to be towed to the rendezvous spot.

JT brought the repair parts, drinking water, and a little food. As soon as he got back to shore, he took a well-deserved nap, only to be awakened and summoned by the mayor of Ushuaia. JT was presented with an award for a superb emergency transfer by the City of Ushuaia.

Sailing again, *Chessie* had a happy crew.

While the repairs to the donkey engine were being finished, *Chessie* managed to shoot off an e-mail to the Living Classrooms Foundation, welcoming the foundation's two special visitors—President Bill Clinton and Vice President Al Gore. "They were very impressed with the technology of the project," said Parker Rockefeller, "especially Vice President Gore." The students at the foundation helped their visitors send a return message, which read, "Thanks for the message. Have a great race. We wish we were with you."

Rick made the repairs as we sailed away. It took them one hour—I timed them—to repair the generator with the spare parts. And it didn't take long to tank up the ballast. The breeze even cooperated. We were a very happy crew!"

Dee explained that "stopping for the replacement parts was the shot in the arm we needed. With the crew revived and the struggle over, we were back in the race. The four musketeers had indeed been caught by the high pressure and were doing only three knots about two hundred miles ahead of us. *Brunel,* near the back of the pack with us, had decided to go east around the Falkland Islands. Because of our stop, we had no choice but to go west of the islands. As we approached the Falklands, it became obvious that we needed to get as far east as possible."

With *Chessie* and *Brunel* charging toward the stalled foursome, the e-mails took on a new flavor. Dalton (*Merit Cup*) and Cape (*Toshiba*) aired some of their frustrations. *Brunel*'s decision to go east of the Falklands and *Chessie*'s improved status after its emergency transfer were infuriating them. "Another frustrating night, totally becalmed at times with the speedo reading zero often for hours on end," wrote Dalton. "Still right alongside *Toshiba,* as we have been now since late yesterday afternoon, but in the daylight we can see what we think is *Swedish Match.*" Dalton's and Cape's e-mails disputed the rendezvous rules and complained about *Brunel*'s high flyer (sailing jargon for big gamble). Would they protest *Chessie*'s emergency stopover? Bryan Fishback and George Collins re-read the rules and consulted with JT. Yes, *Chessie* had stayed within the rules.

Back in Ushuaia, the sleepy town's tempo shifted into overdrive. *Silk Cut* and *EF Education* had arrived. Their repairs were made in record time. *EF Education* set sail, determined to finish the leg, but *Silk Cut* pulled

out of the leg and motored to Brazil with only six crew members, the minimum permitted under race rules. *Silk Cut,* a prerace favorite, had yet to deliver. With this latest catastrophe, skipper Lawrie Smith returned home to convince his sponsors to remain in the race.

Spared the high pressure that enveloped the four musketeers, *EF Language* cruised to a huge first place while a new high approached the fleet from the west southwest. "This would be the decider," remembered Dee. "We had arrived to within 20 miles east of the pack when the foursome finally got some wind. By this time, *Brunel* had developed a 120-mile lead to the east of everyone. *Kvaerner* opted to go east and died a slow death in bad current and headwind. We gybed to get more leverage on the remaining three boats and stay in the strong aft winds longer. It turned into a 120-mile lead over the four musketeers, which we needed for fleet position. With a good lead in place, we went hard after *Brunel.* In two days, we had closed to within 60 miles. The race for second was on.

"The *Chessie* boys pushed the boat hard," Dee said smiling, "while Juan and I worked over the weather and shifts to figure out how to get around *Brunel.* The fast run we had for five days turned into an upwind 500-mile sprint to the finish. Through thunderstorms and wind holes, we continued to gain. During the last 36 hours, we were so close we were worried *Brunel* might see us. If they did, they could put a loose cover on us and prevent us from passing them," he explained. "It became a game of cat and mouse. Then we got a 20-degree wind shift in our favor. We just needed the shift to hold for 60 miles. Unfortunately, it didn't. We managed to close within six miles of the finish, but *Brunel* beat us," Dee explained. "*Chessie* had third."

Chessie played a game of cat and mouse with *Brunel.*

As *Chessie* neared São Sebastião, the shore crew scrounged for an available seaworthy boat. Finally, they convinced some locals to take them out to see the boys in. "Relieved the boys were okay, we were so proud of their comeback," remembered Sally Scott. "As *Chessie* made her way up the channel, the wind died down again, and we watched her drift across the finish line. Talpi waved the American flag enthusiastically for the photojournalists."

Immediately after the dockside award ceremony, Dr. Rudi ushered Greg to the first aid tent to check out his leg. It had not progressed sufficiently; Greg would have to return to Maryland for aggressive treatment if he was going to sail Leg 6. Within hours, Dr. Rudi checked out the entire sailing crew. They had lost quite a bit of weight, but all in all, they were okay. Linda and Laura had their work cut out for them.

The press had many questions for the crew—about breakages, Greg's injury, the emergency stopover, their comeback, and, of course, Dalton's (*Merit Cup*) e-mails. Dee answered the questions in order. As to Dalton's e-mails, he replied, "Sounds like someone who was very frustrated. We've beaten him twice in the Southern Ocean and that says enough."

Dalton's and Cape's (*Toshiba*) e-mails had caused quite an uproar with the Whitbread fans, so much so that Quokka Sports introduced a fan opinion section to their website. Once on shore, Dalton was surprised by the stormy reaction and explained that his complaint was with the rules, not *Chessie*. *Toshiba* and Cape chose to take a low profile. They had more important issues to confront.

During crew declarations, which lasted two and a half hours, the judges interviewed each member of the *Chessie* crew and re-

Top: Chessie drifted across the finish line. She had finished in third place for the third time.
Left: The crew received its award dockside.

Samba time! The crews danced down the crowded street.

viewed the log and digital photos until they were satisfied that *Chessie* had indeed stayed within the rules. When asked, Whitbread Race Manager Michael Woods said, "As for *Chessie's* emergency stop, they made the proper decision." He added, "I would not want to see a rule change that would penalize a skipper for making a proper, seamanlike decision that preserves the safety of his boat and crew."

Chessie was not the only boat receiving close scrutiny. *Toshiba* had used her main engine to remove kelp from her propeller, a major infraction of the race rules. Kelp puts drag on a boat, but the acceptable way to remove it during a race is to stop the boat and have a crew member dive under and dislodge it. *Toshiba* had not done that. Compounding the issue, the crew had not recorded the incident in their log or notified Race Headquarters at the time of the infrac-

tion. Race Headquarters had not learned of it until the presentation of the declarations at the end of the leg. After interviewing the entire crew and reviewing the race rules, the jury ruled against *Toshiba,* disqualifying the yacht from Leg 5. The ruling was a major blow; the boat received no points for the most influential leg of the race.

São Sebastião was in the middle of Carnival, the pre-Lenten festival known as Mardi Gras in New Orleans, and the Whitbreaders were invited to join the festivities. Everyone (except *EF Education* and *Silk Cut,* who were still at sea) sambaed down the main street of São Sebastião. Talpi gave his fellow Chessians a quick samba lesson, but when the music started, they were on their own. By the end of the very long street, the crew had almost mastered the dance and Jon Holstrom was leading the parade.

FINISH POSITIONS
AT SÃO SEBASTIÃO

BOAT	OVERALL STANDING
EF Language	507
Brunel Sunergy	126
Chessie Racing	399
Swedish Match	404
Merit Cup	411
Innovation Kvaerner	372
Silk Cut (resigned from leg)	299
EF Education (resigned from leg)	126
Toshiba (disqualified)	299

Eventually, *Silk Cut* motored into São Sebastião. Lawrie Smith rejoined his crew with good news. Their sponsors would continue their support; *Silk Cut* would remain in the race. With the winds not cooperating, *EF Education* finally gave up, pulled out of Leg 5, and motored toward São Sebastião. *EF Education* and *Silk Cut* would receive 26 points each for completing the leg within the rules. Even motoring, *EF Education* pulled into port only one day before the restart. Her crew was exhausted. The fleet and the entire town came out to greet the ladies, celebrating their courage and determination. Their brother team, *EF Language,* and the shore crew sent the girls into town to eat and rest while they prepared the boat for the next leg.

The Southern Ocean had given the entire fleet a lot to think about. After evaluating the experience, Gavin determined that "it's not how big or strong you are when sailing the Southern Ocean. You need to be smart, know your own limits, and know how to work as a group. Some guys need more sleep or food than others. You have to allow teammates to fill their own needs. Our crew worked well together. We stayed positive and kept our sense of humor. We never gave up!"

São Sebastião, Brazil,
to Fort Lauderdale, Florida

LEG 6

DISTANCE
4,750 nautical miles

START DATE
March 14, 1998

**ESTIMATED
ARRIVAL DATE**
April 2, 1998

After having done Leg 3 in December, Mike Toppa returned to do Leg 6. When he had signed up for this leg a year before, he had had no idea that his wife, Libby, would be expecting twins. "As the date got closer, we realized I probably would be at sea when the twins were born," sighed Mike. Smiling, he continued, "As is typical, Libby was extremely understanding and convinced me that she was comfortable with my not being there. We arranged for plenty of help and support for her in my absence. Everything would be okay. In the meantime, the guys had been back in the Southern Ocean. I had followed them every day via the website and saw them come from behind for a third-place finish in Brazil. I arrived in Brazil knowing they were there by the skin of their teeth and probably a little worn out."

São Sebastião was a tropical paradise—lush green vegetation, sandy beaches, and bountiful fresh fruit. It was also hot, very hot. By noon, the ocean was almost too hot for swimming. "There is a reason the locals take

A lovely beach was situated just beyond the trees.

siestas," said Jon Holstrom. Bryan rearranged the work day to accommodate a two-hour break between noon and 2:00 P.M. "Work started as soon as there was enough light (way too early for most of us!) and ended when we ran out of light (or when we got attacked by the blood-sucking mosquitoes)," remembered Kerry. Some of the crew used the siesta time for surfing and a quick picnic at the beach. Others chose to collapse on nearby hammocks.

Greg returned home to Maryland for aggressive treatment of his leg wound. "There is no way his leg could heal in time for Leg 6 if he remains here," said Dr. Rudi. "The heat and humidity wouldn't let it."

In this small port town, public transportation was meager, and housing and shopping were minimal. Luckily, Carey Swain had found the crew the perfect accommodations. "It was a beautiful setting and a welcome relief from the heat," reminisced Kathy Alex-

ander, "right out of an Ernest Hemingway novel." The entire fleet was envious. "The *Chessie* team and support staff are like a traveling college dorm. Wives, kids, cooks, friends, and shore staff can all be found under the same roof in each port," reported Stephen Pizzo of Quokka Sports. "Here, the team snagged what everyone agrees is the prime piece of coastal real estate, a lovely villa nestled at the end of a long vine-hung jungle road. The *Chessie* dwelling is situated on a private, postcard-perfect, palm-lined, crescent beach." The one thing missing was the *Chessie* children. Because of the water and food warnings, they had stayed with grandparents.

The fleet expected Leg 6 to be a light air leg, especially crossing through the Doldrums. While organizing *Chessie*'s gear for the leg, the crew realized that their lightest spinnaker had mistakenly been put in the wrong container; it was already in Fort Lauderdale.

GREG'S WOUND

Dr. Holt recalled that "Dr. Rudi called me from São Paulo on Saturday to say that Greg had been cut badly on the shin about 10 days earlier, when he was swept aft into a deck fitting by a wave over the bow. The wound had been stapled according to our wound care plan, but not until about 10 hours after the injury, when it had become more infection prone. Dr. Rudi described it as 'pretty ugly.' After taking out the staples and trimming away the infected edges of the wound, he put Greg on a plane back here [Annapolis].

"Greg met me at my house on Sunday afternoon and, after checking the wound, which was wide open and as yet not healing, we went to my office. The wound extended down to the bone," Dr. Holt noted. "I took cultures, washed it out thoroughly, dressed it, and started him on the strongest available antibiotics."

On Monday, Dr. Holt called Dr. Roy Myers, who runs the hyperbaric chamber at the Shock Trauma Center in Baltimore. Dr. Myers agreed to get Greg into the chamber daily that week for treatment with high-pressure oxygen therapy to try to speed up his healing. "On Wednesday, I surgically cleaned and then closed the wound, and I checked it daily afterward," Dr. Holt explained. "Greg continued to go to the hyperbaric chamber every day for his high-pressure oxygen dive, and by Sunday the wound looked like it just might heal. Greg flew back to São Paulo the following day and was cleared for sailing by Dr. Rudi the day before the start.

"All told," Dr. Holt smiled, "it was a remarkably fast recovery from an infected wound down to the shin bone, the most difficult area to heal. I attribute his fast recovery to his care at sea, Dr. Rudi's prompt intervention on shore, and Greg's great health and willingness to cooperate with all the tedious and restrictive care during his brief return to Annapolis."

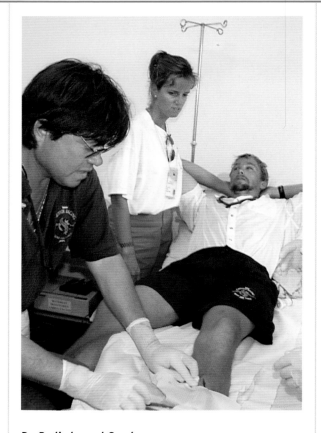

Dr. Rudi cleaned Greg's leg and sent him back to the States for aggressive treatment.

The canopy of trees
provided ample shade
from the scorching sun.

From Brazil, Mike called North Sails Fort Lauderdale and gave them the combination to the container. Six hours of digging through the tightly packed container produced the spinnaker. Without enough time to have it sent by commercial carrier, *Chessie* bought a ticket for Peter Messenger, Florida Rigging, to bring the sail to Brazil. "He ended up having a good minivacation on *Chessie Racing*," quipped Mike.

"It was a tough stopover," remembered Rick. "Brazil was the halfway point of the race; after the race ended, the majority of Whitbreaders would be unemployed. Psychologically, that was a bit of a downer. In addition, *Chessie* needed a lot of work done after Leg 5, and the language barrier slowed us down considerably when trying to get needed equipment. Making matters worse, Brazilians really know how to throw a party, and I haven't met a sailor who can turn down a party. I think the entire fleet was run down

by the time we left the docks," he said with a chuckle and a shake of the head.

In keeping with *Chessie*'s education mission, Kerry and a crew member visited one or two schools at each stopover. In Brazil, Kerry enlisted Talpi, assuming that Spanish was similar to Portuguese. George and Maureen joined them. "It was a lot of fun," smiled Talpi. "We spent about three hours with 20 schoolchildren 9–13 years of age. As Kerry explained who we were and what the Living Classrooms Foundation was, I translated it into Spanish. Somehow the students understood. After that, we jammed through answering questions from students and teachers.

"Their questions were quite diverse. Everyone was concerned about how long we were at sea without seeing our families. The boys' questions revolved around sleep, work, food, and how to become a member of the crew. The girls wanted to know what we

LINDA JONES AS TEAM CHEF: FEEDING THE CREW ASHORE

Some crews had a per diem for meals, but George and Dr. Rudi wanted to guarantee that *Chessie*'s crew ate well-balanced meals. Hired as the team chef two weeks before the race started, Linda knew her way around the sailing world, having been chef for several race syndicates and cruise organizers. After receiving the call from *Chessie,* she had about a week to tie up loose ends and get to Southampton. Being a sailor herself, she wanted to be a part of the Whitbread.

When she arrived at the *Chessie* house in Cowes (on the Isle of Wight, an island off Southampton), she realized that she was starting from scratch. It was 3:00 P.M. and no one had started dinner. She reached for the phone and some car keys. Somehow, she managed to have dinner served at 7:00 P.M. While the crew ate, she took inventory of the kitchen, mulled over recipes, and made her shopping list for the next day. After cleaning up the kitchen, she dragged herself to bed. In the kitchen by 5:30 the next morning, Linda's day had begun. Since the crew was responsible for their own breakfast, she focused on lunch and had it prepared by the time the crew made their way to breakfast. She then hit the stores (butcher, grocer, etc.), delivered lunch to the container, prepared and served dinner, planned the next day's meals, and collapsed into bed about 11:00 P.M. After the first few days being spent negotiating prices for bulk purchases, provisioning the house, and organizing a crew rotation for dinner clean-up, Linda had settled into a routine.

"Fremantle was my best set-up, without a doubt," said Linda. "With each condo facing a central courtyard, I suddenly had seven ovens and stoves available just a short walk away. I set up several large gas grills just outside the kitchen door, which happened to be opposite the *Merit*'s crew condos and resulted in a daily audience come grill time. With a deli-style side-by-side refrigerator, compliments of the local Coca-Cola distributor, and a small tent with tables and chairs for dining just off the living room, it was just fine. I had all the right tools for the job—the first and only time during the entire campaign.

"Then there was Brazil," Linda sighed. "After weeks of advance preparation due to the warnings of dangerous water and food supplies, we arrived to find little ready and a constant steady rain—not a very encouraging start. We quickly realized that the local population was 110 percent behind the effort in preparing for the Whitbread, but we doubted it would ever come together in time. Still, the Brazilian enthusiasm was contagious, and their hospitality was like nothing I have ever seen or comprehended.

"Provisioning was going to require a lot of patience and last-minute menu changes," Linda continued. "Finding the basics was not hard, but beyond that was the unfamiliar. I was told of a new grocery store that would be worth the trip for large provisioning, just an hour and a half away (if you drive daredevil Brazilian speeds). After climbing out of the coastal town, with the road literally eroding away from under us during the daily downpour, our interpreter and I found a very modern, brightly lit, enclosed grocery store. It looked promising and well worth the ride. We grabbed a couple of carts and were off. At checkout, I discovered that the store accepted only cash. Five hours later, I returned with a few bottles of Grey Poupon, some mozzarella cheese, and some very frazzled nerves. Cash is still the best way to do business anywhere in the world, except the States," she laughed.

"One of the best things about Brazilians was their desire to please. No matter what it was you wanted, the answer was 'yes.' The results were something less consistent. 'Yes, the bread you ordered will be ready.' 'Yes, we will have a variety tomorrow.' 'Yes, we can deliver.' In reality, the bread might be ready by noon, the same kind of bread would appear in a different shape, and delivery— it might arrive eventually. Each day was different. Each day a new challenge," she continued. "Provisioning for one day meant stops at no fewer than four food stores or stalls, with some stocked better in the morning and others in the afternoon. As a

Tony Rey, driver, was
born in Washington,
D.C., and learned to sail
when he was eight years
old. He started sailing
professionally in 1995.

result, it might take a couple of trips to town before the day's provisioning was completed."

With a chuckle, Linda went into a little more detail. "Compounding the situation was the heat, the bugs, more bugs, and the cars. Somehow, I seemed to be plagued with the faulty rental car in each port. But in Brazil, as in every other aspect, car problems were larger than life. Not only were they the most expensive cars we rented, but they were the smallest and the least reliable. On one particular day—it was my second rental car in as many weeks—after finishing my midday rounds at the shops and with the car loaded up, it started spitting greasy fluids and coughed up clouds of black smoke. Then it started to sizzle and steam— no, on closer inspection, it was smoke," she exclaimed. "There I was in downtown São Sebastião, unable to speak Portuguese, and the Italian I had used successfully yesterday was of no use today. I ran back to the compound for help. It was pouring rain, the streets were flooded, and our dinner was sitting curbside in a smoldering car! Just another day on the job in Brazil."

The job of chef requires tremendous organizational skills, knowledge of food, and nerves of steel (if you doubt it, try preparing a dinner for 40). It is not for the faint of heart. With endless hours away from the crew, communicating through memos to keep up with the ever-changing schedule, the chef has a very lonely job. Somehow, Linda and Laura managed to put a delicious, well-balanced meal on the table every night and still find time to laugh.

thought of São Sebastião and if I could samba. I told them I had taught my entire crew to samba and demonstrated my technique to prove it," chuckled Talpi. "They treated us to some cakes and fruit juice, which were real tasty. Kerry gave the students the Whitbread Education Program curriculum, and they gave her flowers," he smiled.

John Kostecki had returned as skipper, replacing Dee. Mike Toppa replaced Gavin Brady, and Tony Rey, an Olympic sailor and tactician for the Baird Racing Team, replaced Whirly, who needed to visit an ailing father. Guest spots for the restart were enjoyed by George Collins, Jon Holstrom, and JP (Jon Patton).

Three days before the restart, Greg Gendell rejoined the crew. After holding a quick on-line chat with students from Maryland, he visited Dr. Rudi and passed inspection. The story and the scar were quite impressive, but Greg could sail Leg 6.

Chessie had another hand delivery. After sailing a couple of regattas back to back, Mike had failed to pack his boots. Thirty hours before the restart, he noticed it. "I called my wife, Libby, and she convinced the mayor of Fort Lauderdale, who was coming to see the start, to bring me my boots. The mayor arrived the morning of the race with my duffel bag in hand. Unfortunately, Libby sent the wrong boots—I guess I have too many boots," laughed Mike.

EF chartered a spectator boat; it was packed.

CREW FOR
CHESSIE RACING

LEG

6

John Kostecki, skipper

Juan Vila, navigator

Grant "Fuzz" Spanhake, watch captain

Dave Scott, watch captain/sailmaker

Jerry Kirby, crew boss/bowman

Rick Deppe, bowman

Greg Gendell, bowman

Antonio "Talpi" Piris, trimmer/driver

Tony Rey, driver

Jonathan "Jono" Swain, trimmer/driver

Mike Toppa, driver

Stu Wilson, grinder

March 14—The race started in a narrow channel between São Sebastião and the island of Ilhabella. Mayhem had erupted long before the Whitbread fleet made it to the starting point. Hundreds of spectator boats were jockeying for the best view. Some had even anchored in the middle of the race course, oblivious of the problems they would cause. Further complicating the situation, the Brazilians drove their boats the same way they drove their cars. "Caution was not a high priority," laughed Cary. "It was an absolute free-for-all." Although not all of the boats appeared to be seaworthy, they were there to see the restart.

"It was a zoo," exclaimed Rick, "utter chaos, to the point of being funny. There were boats everywhere and anywhere. It was almost impossible to get through the channel. No boat had an advantage; the problems and frustrations were across the board." As black clouds formed overhead, the spectator fleet reluctantly turned back, and the fleet was on its own. *Chessie* led by a half-mile.

"Oh man," exclaimed Tony Rey, "that first night out of Brazil—what a way to start a boat race! I had gotten the call less than a week earlier to come down from Newport and do Leg 6. Before the start, I had logged a total of four hours on a W60, all in light air, flat-water sail checks out of São Sebastião. The leg started in six to eight knots of breeze, a light air beat [point of sail] around Ilhabella and a mellow reach up the coast of Brazil. I remember thinking, 'These boats are easy. Feels like just another day on the water.'"

On shore, a monsoon struck. Situated between the mountains and the sea, São Sebastião quickly flooded. The narrow channel spread, eventually meeting the first floor of the few hotels and stores. The shore crews scrambled to get everything under cover and tied down. The race office staff struggled to break down the press room and save the computer equipment. Luckily, the computers were located on the second floor of the building, but the wiring continued through the first floor, which was more than knee-deep in water. It was touch and go. "The water came halfway up my thigh when I unsuccessfully tried to rescue one of our rental cars. With numerous critters swimming toward anything that was above water, it was not a pretty sight," recalled Kathy. "I couldn't imagine what was happening aboard *Chessie*."

Back on the water, Tony Rey said, "In the next few hours, two things happened—it got dark and it got windy, really windy." The storm hit, but the guys had become used to sailing in all kinds of weather. "Flooding, what flooding?" asked Rick. "It was just another bad storm, really windy, with lightning and thunder." Dalton e-mailed that the storm "lit up the sky for several hours like bright sunlight. It's a bit worrying knowing that you're one of only nine things sticking up in the area!" The weatherman must have been confused because the forecasted light air, headwind, never materialized. The fleet reveled in 25–30 knots of wind from behind instead.

"It was nearly 2:00 A.M.," remembered Tony, "and I was lying in the top aft bunk, hearing the strangest humming, 'whooshing' noises. Man, with my arms pinned at my sides, I was getting thrown around my narrow platform. Thoughts like, 'This must be what it's like riding an Olympic luge, except it's hot,' kept running through my head. 'What's going on up there?' Suddenly, someone was shaking my leg. 'Okay, time to go boat racing!' I got up and put all sorts of gear on, but it took me a little while because it was dark and I didn't know where the flashlights lived. Everything was wet, and I couldn't seem to stand up without falling over," Tony explained. "Boy, I hated being the new guy!

"Eventually I crawled out on deck, slid the hatch closed behind me, and looked at the illuminated instruments on the mast. Windspeed: 38 knots? Boatspeed: 25 knots? No way; can't be. Then I turned around and looked aft past all the yellow-hooded creatures in the cockpit and saw the rooster tail [high, fountainlike wake] peeling off the transom. The ocean was smoke, and *Chessie* was RIPPING through it. 'Hooo-aah, we ARE doing 25!' I screeched.

"I made my way aft, all hands and knees. Mike was steering. He was in a full-speed tuck, spinning the wheel through his fingers to keep the boat upright and moving; 35–40 knots of wind, Code 3 genaker [cross between a spinnaker and a genoa, which is used for broad reaching], fully tanked, and we were doing powerboat speeds. Time for a watch change, and it was the new guy's turn to drive," Tony continued. "'This is awesome!' I exclaimed. The next four-hour watch

ON-LINE CHAT BETWEEN BOWMAN GREG GENDELL AND STUDENTS OF NORTH CHEVY CHASE ELEMENTARY SCHOOL, MARCH 14, 1998

How did you repair your mainsail?

We repaired the mainsail at sea. It took about three hours. We had six crew members working on it. We have a new one for the next leg. We could have carried a second mainsail with us, but it weighs 220 pounds. We decided that was too much weight, so we only carry one.

Do you think that hypothermia caused your body to not feel any pain when you first cut your leg?

No, I don't think that was it. My body was rushing with adrenaline, and I just did not feel it. It felt like it stung a little and I expected there to be a lump, but I was surprised to find it go the other way—a hole. Jerry Kirby took good care of me. I still have stitches in, and it has been just over one month. The stitches will be coming out a few days after the start.

How big are the staples that were used to close your wound? Did the wound glue work well?

The staples were a little smaller than office staples. We did not use any of the glue.

What is the toughest thing about your job on *Chessie*?

The toughest thing about sailing these boats is the constant work that needs to be done. There is a lot of changing big, heavy sails, and we have to move them around a lot. We also have to do things like trim, grind the winches, and drive, and this stuff is always more difficult at night and in a lot of wind. It would be tough even if we were just going sailing for the day, but we are out there for 30 days! It makes you very tired, and we do not get to sleep much.

What was it like to grow up near the Magothy River?

It was a great place to grow up. In the summer, my brothers, friends, and I would go sailing on big boats and little boats. We had the most fun messing around on lasers, which are 14 feet and built for one person. We would also crab and fish and swim a lot. In the winter, we would go ice skating and play hockey when the river froze up.

Are there any secrets to sailmaking? Our teacher uses a sailor's palm and beeswax thread to repair sails on the *Maryland Dove*. What do you use to repair *Chessie*'s sails?

We use a lot of that same stuff—needle, palm, and whipping twine. We also use a ripstop cloth that has an adhesive back to it. We actually carry a small sewing machine onboard. The day after I got hurt, Stu Wilson and I spent about 15 hours fixing sails. We had a spinnaker that was completely blown into four or five pieces, so we had to patch it up and then sew it.

Are you excited about starting Leg 8 from Annapolis?

The start is going to be incredible. While I was home last week, I got to talk with some people from Annapolis. They are psyched. It should be quite a sight. We are all very excited. The only bad thing is that I will be leaving my home behind for a few more months.

What is the most spectacular form of marine life you have seen while on board *Chessie*?

On the last leg, a few days from the finish, we sailed across a big feeding frenzy. It looked like something from a National Geographic show. There were dolphins everywhere jumping out of the water. There were also marlins that were jumping six to eight feet out of the water. They would spin in circles in the air. There were even sharks that were slowly circling the whole area. We saw a bunch of different birds there also. I think everyone was trying to feed on a big school of fish. It was cool, and we sailed right through it.

Which of the world's oceans is your favorite for sailing, and have you seen much garbage

floating around? Which ocean seemed to be the most polluted?

I like all the oceans. We do not see much garbage in the water. Every few days we may see a soccer ball or a plastic bag or Styrofoam. It is sad to see this. The oceans are vast and beautiful. We would like to keep it that way. On *Chessie* we do not throw anything over. All the Whitbread sailors respect the ocean and keep it clean. If we did not, Mother Nature might come down and kick our butts in the form of a big storm.

When you were in fourth grade, did you ever think that you would get a chance to race around the world?

It was always a dream of mine. I liked sailing and tried to be as good as I could at it. I feel very fortunate to be doing it.

When you get to Baltimore, what is the first REAL food that you would like to eat?

I just got back from a week in Baltimore where I was being treated for my injury. The doctors put me in a hyperbaric chamber twice a day for a few days. The chamber accelerated the healing of my wound, so I would be ready for this next race leg. I wanted a home-cooked meal. My family made me a turkey dinner with mashed potatoes and stuffing, just like Thanksgiving or Christmas. Since my wife, Pam, and I missed these, my parents were making up for it. It was great.

Thank you so much for chatting with us! We are very glad your leg is healing and that you will get to continue racing. We are a group of students from four different classes at North Chevy Chase. All of the classes are watching every day to see what happens in the race. Good Sailing!

Thank you very much for all your nice e-mails. I speak for the whole crew when I say we are looking forward to meeting you at the breakfast on April 24.

was the best mogul run I have ever had. I was whooping like a fool, all hopped up on adrenaline. The rest of the crew seemed happy to be back out racing after two weeks off, but they were used to this sort of action. Stu and Rick were laughing at me, saying things like, 'Check the new guy at the wheel.' I had NO IDEA how fast a sailboat could go until that night!"

Several of the boats encountered trouble with Brazilian fishing fleets. *Brunel* sailed into a net, broached (veered to windward), and had to cut the net, costing them a half-hour. *Chessie*, however, got by unscathed. In fact, as they sailed past one boat, a fisherman pointed to his *Chessie* t-shirt! "Man, these shirts keep showing up everywhere," chuckled Jerry.

The heat continued to climb. Below deck, the temperature approached 110°F. "We are sweating like pigs day and night," wrote Frostad (*Kvaerner*). "The water temperature is around 31°C (88°F), and it's just very, very hot. Our five-liter drinking bottles on deck just get filled up all the time. The worst is when you sleep more than two hours without drinking and wake up completely dehydrated. We push each other to drink all the time, and that definitely keeps the headache away." The heat also played havoc with the food supplies. *Swedish Match* wrote that the chocolate onboard needed to be eaten quickly before it melted. Christen Horn Johannessen (*Swedish Match*) celebrated his 31st birthday with "a whole plate of melted chocolate."

By the third day, *Chessie* was nine hundred miles up the coast and ahead of schedule, with a three-mile lead on the fleet. As she neared the equator, things got tricky. Mike explained that "large squall systems marched over our track, dumping buckets of rain and leaving no wind in their wake. In fact, the wind would do a 360-degree directional

Chessie **sailed through the storm.**

change, causing 10 to 15 sail changes. Two to four hours later, the gradient wind would finally reestablish itself. All the boats were susceptible, but some either knew how to use it to their advantage or were luckier. Our lead diminished, and *Chessie* was passed by a few boats."

The squalls resulted in "parking lots," which ultimately became the great equalizers. *EF Language* and *Kvaerner* called these restarts. As Cayard (*EF Language*) wrote, "You pick your route based on historical data and the forecast, but then micro systems develop and, if they happen along your path, that is too bad."

"It was the beginning of Day 7," remembered Mike, "about 4:00 A.M., when a large squall came through with a lot of wind and rain. I'll never forget it. Rick was on the foredeck setting the staysail when the boat rolled in a wave. He lost his balance, flipped over the lifelines, and was launched over the

side and almost off the boat. I lost sight of him. Fortunately, Rick was able to grab hold of the lower lifeline and hang on until Jono grabbed him and hauled him back on board." As the rain diminished and the wind died, the sun came up. Seven of the boats were lined up, literally bow to bow, and the racing started again.

"Leg 6 was a very demanding leg," recalled Rick. "With the extremely high temperatures, the constantly changing conditions that demanded numerous sail changes, and the closely packed fleet, the pressure was incredible. In addition, it was hot, VERY hot, but the competition remained intense. We sailed very aggressively."

The entire fleet began to write home about the heat and the "spotty bum" they were experiencing. On board *Chessie*, everyone had skin rashes—hives, athlete's foot, spotty bum—but John Kostecki came down with a serious case of hives on his legs. Al-

Top: Hot sailing.
Left: EF Language was
spotted after one of the
many storms.

though he applied salves regularly, it got so bad that Jerry e-mailed Dr. Rudi, who advised John to stay out of the sun and off his feet. Unwilling to stay out of the action completely, John snuck up at night when it was a little bit cooler to see how the crew was doing.

This would be *Chessie*'s second crossing of the equator but the first time for John Kostecki and Tony Rey. Because of John's legs,

the crew decided against having the ceremony. Would King Neptune be upset? Possibly. Things went downhill from there.

"The Doldrums didn't follow the advertisements," explained Mike. "It got light, but we always had wind. Once we got north of the equator, the trick was to know how far into the northeast trade winds *Chessie* should sail and when to start heading west. We got some pretty good shots of wind from the

SKIN PROBLEMS

Gunwale bum (a/k/a spotty botty, skipper's seat, or pepperoni butt) is described as "painful pimples and boils on the affected person's bottom" causing "extreme discomfort when sitting down," explained Alby Pratt (*Innovation Kvaerner*). By whatever name, the malady struck all of the crews.

Although the condition is well known in the sailing community, Dr. Rudi had trouble finding medical documentation on it. "You could get some indication of what it was by what caused it," explained Dr. Rudi. "Close to 20 percent of the fleet had spotty botty or dermatitis of the buttocks area. It usually started from prolonged wetness and friction, as caused by foul weather suits and heat, and it started about two to five days after leaving Brazil." There are home remedies for spotty botty, but the best seems to be reversing the conditions that cause it—exposing it to air and sun and keeping pressure off the affected area.

The sailors also suffered from other skin problems. According to Dr. Rudi, solar keratoses, precancerous lesions due to the sun, affected several of the sailors. The time in the Southern Ocean and Australia (under the hole in the ozone) necessitated the removal of malignant melanomas and other lesions from several sailors. Herpes labialus, or cold sores (an infection of the lips was caused by first- and second-degree sunburn), and, of course, sunburn regularly cropped up. Wide-brimmed hats and zinc oxide proved successful in limiting those ailments. Athlete's foot was another really common problem.

John Kostecki had possibly the worst skin infection, one that traveled up both his legs. The infection started when John was wearing his boots. "Diagnosing his problem was difficult because I had to rely on digital images sent to me by e-mail," remembered Dr. Rudi. "He had little boils all over his legs from the knee down to the ankles, with marked swelling and redness on his legs; after four or five days of antibiotics and staying in his bunk, it started to improve. My best guess was that he suffered from ecthyma, a deeper kind of bacterial

Mike applied sunscreen before going on watch.

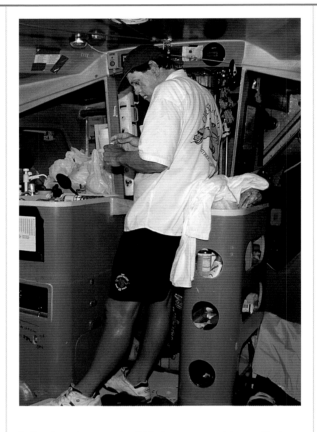

infection. Commonly, kids have something called *impetigo*, which shows up as sort of honey-crusted sores on their faces. Ecthyma is a deeper manifestation of the same strep or staph infection. Actually, ecthyma was one of the most common infections seen in the U.S. Army in Vietnam, among the foot soldiers who were in the rice paddies. Again, the combination of boots chafing the skin, heat, and moisture were the culprits," explained Dr. Rudi.

70- to 50-degree direction, thought we were there, and broke off from the pack."

Unfortunately, the next day the wind went light again and changed direction. While five other boats continued deeper into the trade winds, *Chessie* had been head-faked by the temporary northeast the night before. "This was a rude awakening, as we fell into a 'glue pot,' and *Kvaerner* and *EF Language* sailed around us only a half-mile away," wrote Fuzz.

Chessie had been match racing with *Toshiba* for some time. As Tony remembered, "It was 4:30 P.M. on Day 14, and we had another 140 miles to go before we reached Fort Lauderdale. At present speed, angles, and forecasted conditions, that would put us in the United States sometime midmorning on Tuesday. That fact was particularly difficult to swallow, as the leg winners would have been finished for NEARLY A DAY. John and I talked about how we've lost a lot of boat races before, but never by a full 24 hours. This was the longest race that either of us had done, and it put some past wins and losses into a new perspective."

Cayard (*EF Language*) noted that a new school of "baby flying fish have just been born and they don't fly very well yet. So, as we reach along, they get scooped up in the water that ends on the deck and get in our sail bags, sheet bags, etc. Some even land in your face along with the other four gallons per wave."

Chessie seemed to have found the grown-ups of the school. "One unique hazard on the W60 is flying fish," said Tony. "They move pretty fast, and the occasional one misjudges his trajectory and ends up in the cockpit, flailing around. Last night, Jerry was standing at the grinder pedestal, telling one of his typically entertaining stories, when he was hit in the eye by a 10-inch flying fish. Jerry is a pretty tough guy, but you'd think he had

been hit by Mike Tyson by the way he fell to the cockpit floor. We watched the two of them (the fish and Jerry) flail around the cockpit until the fish flipped its way out of the transom. Jerry finally stood up and shook it off. His eye has been swollen all day, and he's been telling the story ever since," laughed Tony.

Strategy was still the key to ultimate victory. Dalton (*Merit Cup*) wrote that "there are some boats going up, some going down—the big question is which way are we going to try to match them? There's a conference going on in the nav station at the moment . . . It's a time for very sharp tactics."

Since exiting the Doldrums over a week before, *Chessie* had had one frustrating sked report after another. Rick grumbled, "We are pretty frustrated not being in the front of the fleet anymore." Tony wrote home that, "in this race, the rich have gotten richer, and we have been overdrawn on the *Chessie* for most of this leg. However, just because you're poor, doesn't mean you can't be having fun and still racing hard. Our focus right now is to stay ahead of *Toshiba,* currently 1.5 miles dead astern [behind]. For the past three days, we have been going jibe for jibe with her as we match race in rain squalls, big wind shifts, and hot sunshine through the Bahamas and into the Gulf Stream."

As *Chessie* neared Barbuda, *Toshiba* caught up. "We had sailed too low [below the desired course based on wind direction]," explained Mike. "As a result, we had to adjust and sail higher and at a slower angle to get around the flat coral rock. When we cleared the island, we found ourselves bow to bow with Standbridge and his crew. It was close for a while, but we were able to pull ahead and reestablish a one-mile lead." Standbridge (*Toshiba*) wrote, at the same time: "*Chessie Racing* is only half a mile to leeward, neck and neck to the mark. The two boats are very evenly matched, both doing 15 knots average boat speed." Then *Toshiba* started to gain again. What was wrong? Peering through the window at the bottom of the boat, the crew could see that *Chessie* had something wrapped around her keel.

The crew dropped the kite (spinnaker) and shot head to wind to stop the boat. Talpi jumped over the side with a knife, dove down, and cut the thing off. "I thought it was going to take too long, and we'd lose a lot," said Mike, "but we got the chute down quickly. By the time we got Talpi back on board and had another spinnaker up, only about three minutes had elapsed. We were still in front of *Toshiba*." Talpi had cut away 20 feet of thick Brazilian fishing rope.

"The next day was the fastest I had ever gone on a sailboat," Mike continued. "A squall rolled through and the wind picked up

RACE POSITIONS, MARCH 23, 1998

BOAT	NAUTICAL MILES TO LEADER
EF Language	0.0
Silk Cut	1.2
Innovation Kvaerner	19.4
Merit Cup	25.5
Swedish Match	29.6
Chessie Racing	44.9
Toshiba	57.0
Brunel Sunergy	70.6
EF Education	109.5

to about 35–40 knots. The waves were up, and we had the blast reacher and a staysail on. We hit 32 knots as we rolled off one wave!"

The match race with *Toshiba* continued through the remaining days and nights to the finish of the leg. At times, less than a quarter-mile separated the two boats but never more than 10–20 miles. At night, *Chessie* would take bearings on *Toshiba*'s bow lights to measure any change in relative position. *Chessie* had some excellent watches during that time. "We were in total control of the boat," explained Rick. "Stu and I felt like we had mastered her, whizzing past the Caribbean islands at 18 knots. We were in familiar waters, and the United States had never looked so good—high-pressure showers, cold beer, and air conditioning. It would feel soooo good."

As they neared Fort Lauderdale, the phone satcom started to ring more. *Chessie* was five days ahead of schedule, but 24 hours behind the leaders. Since some of the containers had not arrived yet, the shore crew had to scramble, shortening vacations, rearranging flights, and evaluating the repair list to determine what gear was needed. "Each time the phone rang, I was sure it was a message that my wife had given birth, but that message never came," remembered Mike.

The most critical gear problem for this leg was that two of *Chessie*'s computers had crashed, leaving Juan with one computer. "We couldn't receive too much," said Juan. "Most of the information came in on the Satcom B, which could be quite unreliable when it got rough and windy. At times, I couldn't log in to get the weather and determine our options. I just had to wing it."

Chessie and *Toshiba* continued their match race to the finish line. For approximately eleven hundred nautical miles, the two boats were seldom more than a few miles apart. "It

Toshiba and *Chessie* seemed to be attached by a bungee cord throughout Leg 6.

Mike and his family
strolled through Race
Village in Fort Lauder-
dale.

FINISH POSITIONS
AT FORT LAUDERDALE

BOAT	OVERALL STANDING
Silk Cut	399
EF Language	608
Swedish Match	493
Innovation Kvaerner	449
Merit Cup	477
Chessie Racing	454
Toshiba	343
Brunel Sunergy	248
EF Education	148

was fun racing, but we were still pretty disappointed with our fleet position," said Rick.
"As we neared the finish line, the *Merit Cup*
boys came out to cheer us on. It was great,
seeing a boatload of *Merit Cup* boys waving
Chessie flags. It took the edge off our poor
showing," he smiled. *Chessie* finished on
March 30 at about 9:00 A.M. in sixth place,
beating *Toshiba* over the line by 2 minutes 53
seconds. The two boats had missed the spectator fleet experienced by the earlier boats
over the weekend.

"It was great finishing the race in my
home town," said a grinning Mike. "There is
nothing like walking off a W60, having not
showered or eaten anything decent for two
weeks, and going straight to your own
home—and, best of all, the babies had still
not made their entrance." The twins had
waited for Daddy; they were born five days
later.

Fort Lauderdale, Florida, to Baltimore, Maryland

DISTANCE
870 nautical miles

START DATE
April 19, 1998

ESTIMATED
ARRIVAL DATE
April 22, 1998

LEG
7

Chessie was back in the States—reliable air conditioning, no need for currency exchange, English spoken with familiar accents (although the rest of the fleet had trouble understanding some of the new accents), driving on the right side of the road. The crew was home—well, almost. In the United States, *Chessie* was a *hot* commodity. Kathy, juggling two cell phones and a beeper, said that "everyone wanted a piece of us. With Mike on the crew, Fort Lauderdale had adopted *Chessie* as its home team. There were visits to and from schools, radio and television appearances, speaking engagements, yacht club and stopover parties—you name it, we did it. We even had a local fan club, complete with volunteers ready, willing, and able to do our bidding."

For the first time, *Chessie* had a sales booth. In addition to the local volunteers manning the booth, some of her Baltimore volunteers came to Fort Lauderdale to help. One of the Race Village's most popular booths, *Chessie* needed additional paraphernalia shipped to Florida to keep up

Above: The crew quickly realized that being chased by the press in Sydney, Auckland, and São Sebastião was only a training ground for the U.S. stopovers.
Right: Two Baltimore volunteers, Jeanne Fagan and Binnie Bailey, came to Fort Lauderdale to help with the *Chessie* booth.

With their only breaks being when the boats were at sea, shore crews had none during short legs.

with demand. Soon it was difficult to distinguish the crew from its fans. Everyone sported *Chessie* gear.

The days sped by. The sailors struggled to meet all their obligations, and the shore crews tried to prepare the boat for Leg 7 while fans milled around watching and asking questions. Although tiring, it was exhilarating. Chessians began to understand the effect *Chessie* was having on fans across the country. One little girl, who had e-mailed Gavin during Leg 5, traveled all the way from Seattle, Washington, in the hope of meeting him and seeing *Chessie*. Unfortunately, Gavin had flown back to Annapolis to take care of some business. While Kathy gave the girl and her parents a tour of the boat and introduced her to some of the sailors, she received a call from Gavin. "Talk about perfect timing! When I handed her the phone and said

Gavin wants to talk to you, she lit up like a Christmas tree."

Some crews flew ahead to reconnoiter the Baltimore/Annapolis area and do a helicopter tour of the Chesapeake Bay. The crews were used to ocean racing, but the bay, with its shallow shoals, crab pots, fish traps, and fishing boats, was new turf. *Toshiba* even hired a local pilot as crew for the leg. Although *Chessie* was entering her home waters, she had little advantage. Most of *Chessie*'s hometown sailors did their sailing in ocean regattas and seldom sailed in the bay. Warned about the Chesapeake's constantly changing sandy bottom, Juan and John flew ahead to check it out, too. What once was 13 feet deep could now be 6 feet deep. The W60s, drawing 12.5 feet, had to know where they could fit. Staying clear of crab pots and fishing areas, which could be moving targets, also concerned the sailors, especially since the deep W60 keels

The W60s lined up at the dock in Fort Lauderdale.

CREW FOR CHESSIE RACING

LEG

7

George Collins, skipper

Juan Vila, navigator

John Kostecki, tactician

Grant "Fuzz" Spanhake, watch captain

Dave Scott, watch captain/sailmaker

Jerry Kirby, crew boss/bowman

Gavin Brady, driver

Greg Gendell, bowman

Antonio "Talpi" Piris, trimmer/driver

Jonathan "Jono" Swain, trimmer/driver

Paul "Whirly" van Dyke, trimmer/driver

Stu Wilson, grinder/sailmaker

seemed to be magnets for all kinds of obstacles. *Chessie* certainly did not want anything slowing her down as she sailed home.

At each port, the shore crews participated in their own race, one against the clock. They unpacked the containers and distributed the sailors luggage; organized the offices; obtained the needed supplies; met the boats; repaired the boats; attended the required social functions, team meetings, and Whitbread meetings; crewed the chase boats; and quickly repacked the container. In addition, they ran errands, talked to fans and the press, and even helped entertain the children following the boats. When the boats left, the shore crews took a deep breath. Their race was over.

When the legs lasted 10 days or more, the shore crews could take a few days to tour the area or take a short side trip. When the legs were less than 10 days, the shore crews

promptly boarded a plane to the next port so they could start all over again. The job, typically consisting of three to four weeks straight followed by one or two weeks off, could become six to fifteen weeks straight without a day off.

George was back on the boat for this leg; Rick would sit this one out. The restart guests would be George's sons, Jack and George.

April 19, the start of Leg 7, had arrived. It was a glorious day, with sunny skies and 20- to 25-knot winds. The spectator boats came out in force, and *Chessie* was on her way home! Everyone would be glued to their website for the next few days, except the fans who would be waiting at the mouth of the Chesapeake to welcome *Chessie* home.

"It was a great start," exclaimed George, "so many people, so many boats, so much excitement. The Whitbread had come to the States, and the interest came with it. Conner

was back onboard *Toshiba* for this leg, and he was playing hardball. While we were getting into position, he nosed ahead of us and *Kvaerner* just before the start, boxing out a number of boats, including *Chessie*. He was preventing us from tacking, and *Chessie* and *Kvaerner* found themselves on a short tack heading into the Committee Boat. Now, the last thing I wanted to do was hit that Committee Boat. I had just met the captain and his crew the night before, and they were nice guys. Besides, I didn't want to crash a $3 million boat." At the last minute, Conner tacked and *Chessie* and *Kvaerner* were able to turn in time. The wind was good, and the race was on.

"Leg 7 started with a bang for us, as we led the fleet out of Fort Lauderdale," remembered Greg Gendell. "Everything was going well; things were clicking. John led Gavin at the helm for a great send-off, and the rest of

Chessie's fans gave her a rousing send-off. Some hefty bets were placed on how many hits the website would receive as the boats raced toward the finish line in Baltimore. In Auckland, the total had reached more than 13 million. Could the Baltimore finish top that? It did—14 million hits in a 24-hour period.

Chessie and *EF Language* maneuvered for position.

Left: By the first mark,
Chessie was in the
lead. Her fans may have
been seasick, but they
were happy.
Bottom: Toshiba boxed
out *Chessie* and *Kvaerner*.

Chessie **raced up the Florida coast.**

the crew did a great job getting us out of there. Then things went downhill.

"We went to turn on our water maker that night and no dice. Jerry inspected it and reported that the cat-pump was cracked. It had just been serviced in Fort Lauderdale!" exclaimed Greg. "We were back to rationing water; luckily, it was a short leg." The people who serviced the donkey engine in Fort Lauderdale had filled the oil level to the mark of a power boat. When the boat heeled over, the oil rushed out and caused the cat-pump to break.

Out came the hand-held water makers, and the crew began pumping. "Forty pumps per minute, every pump producing two drops of water," moaned Greg. "We had one cooked meal and only two cups of water a day. Dehydration and hunger again became a factor." After tasting the hand-pumped water,

George had a better understanding of what the boys had gone through in Leg 5. "Water from a plastic, hand-held water maker does not taste very good," he grimaced. "You have to be very thirsty to drink plastic."

The wind grew to 40 knots right on the nose, banging the fleet against the Gulf Stream and making the seas very rough; however, it did not dampen the enthusiasm. Most of the fleet could have used some Dramamine. Big, lumpy seas and waves without backs stayed with the fleet until Cape Hatteras.

Between the broken water maker and the rough seas, *Chessie*'s concentration was not totally on sailing. "It is not an excuse, but it was a factor," explained Greg. "Hindsight is always 20/20," grumbled George, "but that night, *Chessie* made her first tactical error. She stayed inside the [Gulf] Stream too long." *Brunel* sailed right through it and gained 20 miles on the fleet. "Our hats were

Toshiba and *Chessie* still
seemed to be attached
by a bungee cord.

off to them; they did a great job!" said Greg, grimly.

Kranz (*Swedish Match*) agreed, "*Brunel,* what a killer. Gutsy and definitely a big move. If they pass the front without too much of a stop, they will possibly make it." Cayard (*EF Language*) also applauded the move, "*Brunel* has made a bold move to run east of the Stream and the cold eddies that have adverse current."

The rough seas accompanying the fleet north gave it a beating. "I think you are looking at one tired fleet," wrote George. "Most of the day has been spent scaling 12-foot moguls. For this 57-year-old sailor, there is only so much up and down smashing into waves at 10 knots I can take. I can't wait for the friendlier confines of the Chesapeake Bay. This is worse than that Fastnet." Frostad (*Kvaerner*) wrote: "With about four knots of current against the wind, the waves are just

big and steep. Sometimes you fly in your bunk, and you just wonder what is going to break when you land." Dalton concurred, "The motion is uncomfortable and the noise is tremendous. Sitting on the rail seems an attractive alternative to being tossed out of a bunk."

As the lead boats entered the bay, they noted the water temperature dropping, the seas flattening a little, and the scenery changing. The crews began layering their clothes to keep warm. "Does not really look like a Whitbread, sailing so close to land, but I suppose it is all in the game," wrote Heiner (*Brunel*).

"When the sun came up at the Bay Bridge/Tunnel, *Toshiba, Merit Cup,* and *EF Education* were about a mile and a half behind us," Greg remembered. Because of the water problem and a concern over conserving the fuel needed to shift the water ballast,

Chessie raced ahead of the local speedboats.

Chessie sailed conservatively. A tacking duel could deplete the fuel quickly. "*Toshiba* and *Merit* ground us down. We never saw *Merit* again, but we stayed close to *Toshiba* and prepared for another battle to the finish," he recalled.

George and Kathy had warned the crew that the Whitbread and *Chessie,* in particular, had taken Baltimore and Annapolis by storm, but the crew had dismissed it as hype. "It wasn't until we saw the first airplane 150 miles out from the Chesapeake Bay Bridge/Tunnel and a small Boston Whaler police boat at the mouth of the Potomac and then had hundreds of boats following us by the time we reached Annapolis that all of us onboard realized this would be a special stopover for the Whitbread fleet," exclaimed Dave. George piped in, "The boats actually began meeting us before we even got to the bay. It was amazing! Hundreds tried to follow us,

but we were doing 10–12 knots, and most of them couldn't keep up and they'd drop out. Still, numerous boats stayed with us all the way up the bay!"

As the two boats neared Poplar Island, *Toshiba* went inside a channel marker. "I may be from Barcelona, Spain, but I don't think you can take a W60 in there," Juan smiled. He was right. Conner ran aground, and George smiled as *Chessie* sailed by her. Unknowingly, *Toshiba* had just won the Gibson Island Yacht Squadron's Grounding Award, presented each year to the first boat to run aground in the Chesapeake Bay, and *Toshiba* was the very first W60. As a member of the club, George could not wait to present the award to Dennis Conner.

April 22—The match race between *Toshiba* and *Chessie* that had begun in São Sebastião was still on. "Right off Annapolis, *Toshiba* had her whomper up. We had our Code 3

The Chesapeake Bay
Bridge—the boys were
coming home.

Overleaf: Almost there,
Chessie sailed under the
Bay Bridge.

LEG 7

172

Right: George took the
helm.
Bottom: Parker and
the *Chessie* wives went
out to meet the crew.
Over the roar of the
engine, Kathy manned
the phones and reported
the finish.

Left: Toshiba beat *Chessie* by nine seconds. *Bottom:* A disappointed crew sailed into Baltimore's Inner Harbor.

With the sun setting,
Chessie motored into the
harbor.

The press greeted
George at the dock.

The fans brought smiles
to the crew.

spinnaker up and weren't going to make the center span of the Bay Bridge," said Greg. "When we dropped the Code 3, *Toshiba* passed us. Sailing into the Patapsco, we had a gybing dual with *Toshiba* all the way to the finish. Twenty gybes to the finish, and *Toshiba* beat us by nine seconds!" he said, shaking his head as he remembered. A broken sheet line at the finish did not help.

"We were very disappointed. We let ourselves down but, more important, we felt like we had disappointed all of our supporters," Greg continued. "With long faces, we started motoring toward the Inner Harbor." There were people on spectator boats, on the shorelines of Fort McHenry, on the docks of Canton—people were everywhere cheering *Chessie!* "When we looked around, we were astonished! Everyone was still cheering us, regardless of our finish! We realized they were congratulating us for what we had accom-

plished during the entire Whitbread, and we tried to forget about this finish," Greg said smiling. "Baltimore gave us a great reception."

Strong support from the hometown fans overwhelmed everyone. Banners hung from the skyscrapers said, "Go *Chessie,*" "We love you, *Chessie,*" and "Welcome Home Sailors." Swarms of people lined the Inner Harbor wall and crowded the balconies; they were on rooftops and hanging out windows. It seemed like everyone was there to welcome home *Chessie.*

As the crew climbed off the boat and made their way to the stage, the noise was deafening. *Tubthumper* was being played over the loud speakers, and everyone was clapping and singing along. Keith Mills, a local television sportscaster, had a tough time settling down the crowd to ask George a few questions and officially welcome the crew, but

Fans welcomed the
Whitbread to Baltimore.

FINISH POSITIONS

BOAT	OVERALL STANDINGS
Brunel Sunergy	353
Swedish Match	585
EF Language	689
Innovation Kvaerner	519
Silk Cut	459
Merit Cup	527
Chessie Racing	494
EF Education	178
Toshiba	363*

*After *EF Education* won a protest against *Toshiba,*
Toshiba lost two positions.

when George started to talk, the crowd immediately went silent. With a mixture of disappointment and pride on his face, George tried to convey his thoughts. "I'm relieved and disappointed, but it's great to be home!" he said. "It's so good to see some familiar faces, so many faces. You are terrific! Fans, like you, make the struggles we've encountered worth it. Thank you." And, with a little chuckle, he added, "And it's good to see more *Chessie* and Oriole hats and fewer Yankee hats." The crowd went wild.

Annapolis, Maryland, to La Rochelle, France

DISTANCE
3,390 nautical miles

START DATE
May 3, 1998

ESTIMATED
ARRIVAL DATE
May 16, 1998

LEG
8

The first piece of business in Baltimore was determining the protest *EF Education* filed against *Toshiba* for a nighttime port/starboard incident on Leg 7. While traveling after dusk, the race rules clearly stated that boats must use their running lights and signal turns. *Toshiba* had failed to do so. Quick reactions on *EF*'s part had prevented a near collision, and a protest was filed. The Whitbread judges grilled the two teams during declarations; the ruling went against *Toshiba*, penalizing the boat two finish positions. Guillou (*EF Education*) said that she was "happy with the decision of the jury. For me, the rule for collisions at sea is not only a racing [rule] but also a safety rule." As a result, *Chessie* moved up from eighth to seventh. *Toshiba*'s navigator, Andrew Cape, resigned, and after some scrambling, *Toshiba* hired navigator Murray Ross for the final two legs.

The Baltimore/Annapolis port of call was shared between two cities, which made it quite unique. It was spring, and the Whitbread was in

Over a half-million fans
visited the Whitbread
Race Village in Balti-
more.

town. Welcoming the fleet like no other port, Baltimore/Annapolis's overall attendance surpassed even Auckland's; over a half-million people visited Race Village in Baltimore during the eight-day stopover, and another sixty thousand visited Race Village in Annapolis during its three-day stopover period. Under beautiful, sunny skies, fans milled around Race Village in Baltimore's Inner Harbor. The entire fleet found local interest and knowledge of the race surprising. Such interest was expected in New Zealand but not in the United States, where the Whitbread was relatively new. The Whitbreaders immediately felt at home.

With music, children's activities, and food, Baltimore's Inner Harbor came to life, but the main attractions were the boats and the sailors. Answering a common complaint that the boats were too far away to be seen, Jon Holstrom explained, "You can't bring these boats too close to shore. It's not deep enough." The floating dock, donated by Eastern Floatation and Baltimore Marine Center, was very sturdy, so the Race Village organizers set up a tour to let small groups go down to see the W60s up close. The line wrapped around the harbor; people waited for over an hour to view the boats up close. Still, the fans could not board the boats. The crews had too much work to do. The custom of docking the boats in the order they finished caused a second complaint. *Chessie* had not done well and was near the back. To satisfy the fans, the port organizers switched *Chessie*'s slip to the front, where she could easily be viewed. Her fans happily clicked away through rolls of film.

Chessie had a booth again, and it sold out of paraphernalia daily. The entire city looked like a *Chessie* camp. Maryland Screenprinters, one of *Chessie*'s supplier sponsors, remained open every night to make sure that t-shirts,

Left: George stopped to sign a few autographs for his young fans. *Right:* Shoes lined the dock when George opened *Chessie* to hundreds of lucky fans, who gasped at the "crummy" accommodations below.

Kathy Alexander demonstrated crew jobs to students.

hats, and other *Chessie* gear were available each day. "Someone tried to buy my *Chessie* hat for $50," laughed Steve Smith, *Chessie*'s lead volunteer. "I guess I should have sold it, but I wasn't sure I'd be able to get another one."

Families had come from all over to be a part of the race they had followed on the Internet. "A teacher from New York showed up," remembered Rick. "His classes had been following the race, so I gave him a tour of the boat." Schools took field trips to see the Whitbread fleet. "There were so many kids there we couldn't unload the boat," chuckled Jon Holstrom, "so I put them to work." Hundreds of schoolchildren chanted "*Chessie, Chessie*" while they waited their turn to walk down the pier and see *Chessie.* Jon recruited some boys to carry one of the big sails and told them to take it to the container (*Chessie*'s traveling workshop). He then turned to some

girls and asked, "Are you going to let them show you up?" They carried the next sail. While the schoolchildren unloaded *Chessie,* the Inner Harbor rocked with "*Chessie, Chessie.*" The children were in their glory as they carried off the 17 sails, the sleeping bags, the trash bags, and more. Other crews tried to recruit *Chessie*'s young helpers and alter the chant, without success. After waiting in line to see the W60s and meandering through the Race Village, the fans sat on the stands at Rash Field, overlooking the container park, and watched the shore crews at work.

Interviews, sponsor visits, parties, luncheons, school visits, and guest appearances on television and radio were the norm. "There was something to do every minute," said George. "I didn't have a minute to myself; none of the crew did. The packed schedule in Fort Lauderdale seemed mild compared to Baltimore/Annapolis."

Maureen Collins (*left*) and George (*right*) reluctantly presented Grant Dalton (*center*) and the crew of *Merit Cup* the City of Baltimore's award for the fastest time up the bay. "This was supposed to go to *Chessie*," George chuckled as he and Dalton shook hands.

At the Skippers' Luncheon, George and Bill Boykin, D-Day veteran and former commodore at the Gibson Island Yacht Squadron, presented the squadron's Grounding Award to Bill Trinkle, *Toshiba*'s team manager. With a big grin on his face, George said, "It is with great pleasure that I present this award to you and Dennis Conner. Welcome to the Chesapeake."

On April 30, the crews packed their containers and headed down the road to Annapolis. Receiving a warm send-off from Baltimore and the local fans, *Chessie,* with Walter Cronkite on board and Maureen Collins at the helm, followed by the Whitbread fleet, led Baltimore's Second Annual Parade of Sail. "I was waiting for them in the bay," said a local boater, "but my power boat couldn't keep up with them." Beckley (*EF Education*) wrote: "Accompanying us today down the upper Chesapeake were scores of small crafts, some tall ships,

patrol boats, yachts, jetskis, etc. As we neared the William P. Lane Memorial Bridges (better known as the Chesapeake Bay Bridge), the crowd of craft swelled to welcome us to Annapolis—America's Sailing Capital." In addition, the shorelines, the Naval Academy wall, the docks, the rooftops, and the balconies were overflowing with fans. They were everywhere. Despite overcast skies, Annapolitans demonstrated their love of *Chessie* and sailing with much gusto.

"The next day the skies opened up. It not only rained, it poured," said JP, "but that didn't keep the crowds away." Over the next three days, more than 60,000 people braved the weather to experience the Whitbread firsthand. Again, the *Chessie* booth sold out daily. "We couldn't keep it stocked," chorused *Chessie*'s volunteers.

There were interviews, sponsor visits, parties, and guest appearances every day the

Top: The Orioles wel-
comed the Whitbread
fleet. George was given
the honor of throwing
out the opening ball.
Bottom: Gavin Brady
(right) traded team
hats with Oriole Brady
Anderson (left).

Top: Scores of small craft accompanied the fleet. The Annapolis Yacht Club Junior Sailing Team designed a "baby *Chessie*" to greet their heroes. *Bottom:* Fans packed the seawalls of Annapolis.

fleet was in Annapolis, too. One of the big parties, the Eastport Yacht Club party, was open to the public, with the Whitbread crews as the guests of honor. *Chessie's* crew members arrived by boat. As they disembarked, an unrelenting roar went up. Outdoors in the pouring rain, more than six thousand revelers, ankle deep in mud, were there to celebrate *Chessie* and the Whitbread. They cheered as each crew was introduced. A deafening cheer went up when *Chessie's* crew was brought on stage. After the introductions, the party continued into the wee hours of the night, with dancing and talk of sailing. The rain never let up; neither did the partygoers.

The sun finally decided to show its face for the restart on Sunday, May 3. Maryland's senators, its governor, and the mayors of Baltimore and Annapolis visited *Chessie* and wished her crew a safe and fast trip across "the Pond" to France. As the fleet prepared to return to sea, bagpipes played and the arch-

bishop of Baltimore, Cardinal William Keeler, blessed the fleet. People packed the harbor. If there was a place to stand, whether solid ground or something that floated, there was someone on it.

The fleet's route would retrace its path down the Chesapeake Bay before crossing the northern Atlantic. It would be no easy task. "After sailing *Chessie* from Newport to Southampton last July, I knew the crew needed young, strong, agile men for this leg. I no longer fit that description," George said reluctantly. Rick Deppe returned as one of *Chessie's* bowmen.

Chessie was the third boat to leave the dock, as the boats departed in reverse order of their finishes in Baltimore. "It was good to be back on the boat," said Rick. "The stopover was great, but we needed some rest." Last to leave the dock was *Brunel Sunergy.* As a token of their appreciation for a great stopover, her crew wore t-shirts, each with a

Gloomy weather did not darken the fans' enthusiasm.

Above: Annapolitans stood in lines for hours to view the W60s.
Left: Young *Chessie* fans showed their favoritism.

The crew said good-bye to their loyal followers.

CREW FOR CHESSIE RACING

LEG

8

John Kostecki, skipper

Juan Vila, navigator

Grant "Fuzz" Spanhake, watch captain

Dave Scott, watch captain/sailmaker

Jerry Kirby, crew boss/bowman

Gavin Brady, driver

Rick Deppe, bowman

Greg Gendell, bowman

Antonio "Talpi" Piris, trimmer/driver

Jonathan "Jono" Swain, trimmer/driver

Paul "Whirly" van Dyke, trimmer/driver

Stu Wilson, grinder/sailmaker

different letter. When they stood together, it was supposed to spell THANK YOU USA on one side and FROM HOLLAND on the other. "A few letters were out of place, but they were waving their American flags in earnest," laughed Kerry, "and we got the point."

Looking back at the harbor, one saw a sea of masts, backed by the beautiful historic buildings of Annapolis. The U.S. Coast Guard, in an attempt to maintain control, had laid out a seven-mile-long by one-mile-wide exclusion zone. When the fleet arrived at the start area, they were greeted by a spectator fleet never before imagined. Six thousand to seven thousand boats lined the course. The majority of the boats flew the *Chessie* flag. "As far as the eye could see down the bay, a big wide space was bordered by fluttering green flags," noted Kerry. In addition, 60,000 participants of the annual Bay Bridge Walk watched from the bridge and

The crew of *Brunel Sunergy* attempted to show their appreciation.

another 25,000 fans watched from the shoreline at Sandy Point State Park.

As the fleet paraded to the starting line, the Concorde buzzed low over the fleet and headed straight down the bay. When *Chessie* sailed under the bridge, heading north for the start line, onlookers rushed from one side to the other, cheering and waving as she came out the other side. "It was one of the most exciting moments of the race," smiled Maureen Collins, *Chessie*'s prestart helmsperson. *Chessie*'s other guests for this restart were Ray McCrillis, the sailing team captain at the U.S. Naval Academy, and George Collins.

BANG! Leg 8 got under way a mile north of the Chesapeake Bay Bridge. The fans began cheering as *Chessie,* with Gavin at the helm and John calling tactics, was the first across the line, tacking just in front of *Innovation Kvaerner* and port tacking the fleet to win the start. *Chessie* and *Toshiba* took the

right side of the course, battling it out to pass under the bridge first. *Toshiba,* flying her windward reacher genoa (a sail much larger than the standard W60 jib), had good speed and took the lead. She also took the wind from the fleet. *Swedish Match,* keeping in the middle, stayed away from the spectator fleet.

A strong current was coming up the bay, and *Chessie* and *Toshiba* stayed right to avoid it. As the current went slack, *Swedish Match* took advantage of the better breeze in the middle of the course and passed them. The 6- to 10-knot southwesterly wind slowly increased and shifted east as the boats headed south.

The exclusion zone allowed the sailors a wide berth in which to start the race, but it eliminated much of the excitement and typical chaos that accompanied the restarts. The spectator fleet obediently followed the W60s down the bay to Thomas Point Light, where a wall of boats waited and the exclusion zone

Top: Chessie port tacked the fleet and won the start.
Right: Maneuvering for the start, Juan kept time.

ended. The crews took a deep breath and prepared to do battle. "Just before the gate at Thomas Point, *Chessie* and *Brunel* were neck and neck, with *Brunel* forcing *Chessie* to head west away from the gate [the end of the zone]," explained Kerry. "*Swedish Match* was first through the gate at Thomas Point, followed closely by *Toshiba*, *Brunel*, and *Chessie*, just three seconds later."

The majestic W60s were suddenly lost in a sea of boats, packed with cheering people. Although flooding in from all directions, the spectator fleet consistently made way for the Whitbread racers. *Chessie* had chartered three boats for this restart, and these family boats joined in, with the kids yelling, "Go *Chessie!*" With the sun beginning to set and the wind light and shifty, George and his guests disembarked and headed for land. "They didn't need the extra weight," explained George. "We were only slowing them down."

"The start was fantastic!" smiled Jerry. "Gavin and John decided to port tack the whole fleet and pulled it off. After that, it was all hands on deck until dawn the next day." *Chessie* had passed *Brunel* and was making gains on *Toshiba* and *Swedish Match*. By the time they entered the Atlantic Ocean, *Chessie* led, winning the City of Annapolis trophy for the first out of the bay. George and the crew looked forward to receiving it in La Rochelle. Now alone, the boats sent e-mails to the Whitbread website raving about the Baltimore/Annapolis stopover. The praise continued throughout the leg. "We were so proud of our hometown port," smiled Rick and Greg. The rest of the crew nodded their agreement.

John Kostecki explained the mood on *Chessie*. "We had to redeem ourselves after our poor finish in front of our home crowd, so the pressure was on! Also, Leg 8 gave us a good opportunity to get back in the hunt for

John called tactics, Gavin drove, and the crew trimmed for optimum speed.

Chessie sailed under the Chesapeake Bay Bridge.

the top three or four in overall standings. We sailed extremely well the first night out, but the leg was far from over. Racing into the Gulf Stream, we lost a little to our competitors. It was Code 0 conditions, and our Code 0 was less than ideal," said John. Whirly agreed, "Our whomper was not developed enough." Compounding the problem, all of *Chessie's* sails had started to show wear.

During the stopover in Baltimore, school-children had asked about sharks. Jerry was now on the lookout for them. "For all the school kids that asked about sharks and other wildlife, we saw more sharks last night at dusk than we have seen the entire race. Some were over 20 feet long, with huge dorsal fins," wrote Jerry. "It looked like a scene from *Jaws.* They were feeding on the large schools of fish at the edge of the Gulf Stream."

In fact, spotting wildlife was one of the few forms of entertainment onboard a W60.

Frostad (*Innovation Kvaerner*) commented on seeing many more whales in this Whitbread than in the previous one. *Silk Cut* wrote, "Just woke up to be told we just flew past a very docile sperm whale by some five feet or so! Apparently, Neal Helming saw the group of four whales but was very surprised to see number five appear at the last moment." *EF Education* also "had a small altercation with a whale yesterday. Some fast action on the helm by Leah [Newbold, watch captain] avoided a collision, but the obviously irate cetacean slapped its tail on the water so vigorously that everyone in the cockpit got a shower!" Other wildlife visited the fleet as well. *EF Language* had a run-in with a shark, writing that "another man in a gray suit was stuck to the keel," and *Merit Cup* needed to unwrap "Sammy Seal" from her keel. And, of course, the ever-present flying fish made their entrance. As John wrote, "I got slimed! It was

E-MAILS
FROM OTHER BOATS

EF Education: The city of Baltimore has done the Whitbread Race proud, with huge crowds of interested people visiting the Inner Harbor. We've had a great stopover, with superb Maryland hospitality. Annapolis and Baltimore sure gave us a great send-off yesterday. An unbelievable number of boats of all shapes and sizes took to the water, following us down the course until darkness fell. (Beckley)

EF Language: I am very proud, as an American, of the interest shown in Baltimore and Annapolis for this race and our sport. As many as 250,000 people on the docks per day is nothing to sneeze at for any sport. Neither is 14 million hits per day on the Internet site. (Cayard)

Kvaerner: What a great start outside Annapolis. Never have we seen that many spectator boats. This was definitely a big day for sailing, especially for the Whitbread and sailing in America. (Frostad)

Merit Cup: Well done to the stopover organizers; it was a great stopover. (Dalton)

Silk Cut: A dreary gray Friday here in Annapolis hasn't dampened the enthusiasm of the American public, who are here in their thousands. It is great to see such support and interest in the Whitbread fleet. The start is going to be immense, and all we can say to everyone watching is a big thanks for your hospitality and support. (Stead)

Swedish Match: I want to start with thanking the local organizers and all other people involved in making the Baltimore/Annapolis stopover such a successful and memorable event. (Krantz)

Toshiba: Another great stopover, or two. Thanks to everyone in Baltimore and Annapolis, and an even bigger thank you to the impressive and very disciplined spectator fleet that came out to see us off. (Standbridge)

like getting hit by a baseball while you are standing at bat."

On May 5, Whirly commented on the weather: "It is very warm, almost uncomfortable. Six boats are in sight, so we'll see what happens. We're power reaching, not our fastest point of sail."

An e-mail from *Chessie* described a "crewman's view" of the Whitbread. "We have been sailing along for the past three days quite heeled over (about 15 degrees), which poses many problems to daily living aboard any boat, not just a W60," wrote Dave Scott. "The biggest problem with heeling is moving around inside the boat, without any external references. You have no idea which way the boat will move next.

"A W60 has an aggressive motion at the best of times; however, we are at the moment blast reaching in the Gulf Stream, which I can say with some authority is a very bouncy

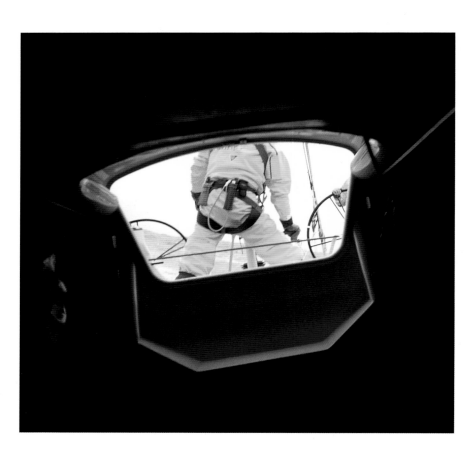

View from below deck. "Most of Day 2, all the boats headed for the Gulf Stream with their whompers up. These sails have some incredible loads on them, so when you hit chop, you just hold your breath," explained Jerry Kirby. "Late in the afternoon, we blew out the spectra strop that holds our whomper up, so it was all hands on deck to fix that problem. A couple of hours after that, the shackle holding our whomper to the bow exploded."

piece of water. The worst thing is when you take off your boot to pull on pants or socks. The boat heels, you slide with an annoying certainty toward the three-inch-deep puddle that our boat has permanently. Your dry socks are now wet for the rest of the trip, unless you are wearing rocky socks (Goretex).

"Cooking, which is a messy job on a good day, leaves you looking like a three-year-old and the galley as though a small incendiary device went off in the beef Stroganoff. I will not go into detail regarding the toilet, except

to say it is a real pain. Stu and I spent three hours down below today repairing a broken headsail after wrestling with the wet sail, rigging up the machine, and getting covered in spray glue," Dave finished.

"We did not play the [Gulf] Stream as well as we should have. We made a mistake by not going fast toward the north and out of the Stream," explained John. Rick recalled the frustration: "I can remember going below and seeing Juan with his head in his hands. After that, we didn't see Juan for a couple of days. He had holed up in the nav station, trying to find a way to recover."

With a high pressure forming, the navigators and skippers poured over weather reports and charts. "We are trying to beat the high pressure on the north side and hope the boats further south will get less wind as they sail closer to the center of the high," wrote Krantz (*Swedish Match*). Standbridge (*Toshiba*) explained, "We have done about one thousand miles with about twenty-five hundred to go. Our major tactical hurdle is the high-pressure system that has been blocking the fleet's path. We are heading into the center, but as we approach, it should get pushed south."

While strategy was the priority of the skipper and navigator, the crew dealt with the breakages. According to Rick, "A day does not go by that something doesn't break on a W60, but there were no major breakages [on Leg 8]," he smiled.

On May 7 Whirly wrote: "Disastrous six hours. We lost 20–25 miles to everyone except *Silk Cut*. Both of us are off. Let's hope the comeback is big. Man, oh man, do we need the guys in front to park, or we don't have a chance." Compounding the problem, wrote Jerry, "right now we have six crew members with either a cold or the flu, although everyone is fighting through it and doing fine."

The crew tried to maintain good spirits,

Top: Jerry categorized the sailing as "Full Metal Jacket conditions. You needed survival suits, harnesses, rubber gloves, Aquaclavas, and goggles to stay on deck."
Left: Sailing through the northern Atlantic was very rough and very wet. Designed for total immersion, the survival suit kept the crew drier, but nothing remained completely dry.

sending home e-mails with silly photos and telling the fans not to worry. Rick recalled that "suddenly Juan appeared in the galley. He was actually chirping while he made some coffee." "We are going to win this leg," said Juan, grinning from ear to ear. Rick wondered what was in Juan's coffee. *Chessie* was three hundred miles behind.

John and Juan consulted and then announced the game plan. *Chessie* would head north after the restricted zone, into iceberg territory. "An iceberg was spotted on the radar, and Gavin, never having seen one before and [*Chessie*] being so far behind, wanted to find it, but Fuzz stopped him," chuckled Rick. "In addition to being dangerous, we were in a race, and Juan had another one of his plans."

Whirly described the conditions in his log as "very, very wet with 35–40 knots of wind and we're full on. We are the northernmost boat. Let's hope it pays off with more wind."

Juan predicted that "the high pressure that is forming off the European coast is going to turn the rest of the fleet into a parking lot. We will have less of that to sail through." The crew agreed that the North Atlantic was tough sailing, very cold and very wet. "This leg had fire hose conditions," exclaimed Rick. "It was without a doubt the wettest leg. The crew wore their survival suits most of the time."

The plan worked. Coming into La Rochelle, *Chessie* had passed most of the fleet, securing a safe third. "There was no way we could make second, but after being three hundred miles back for a good portion of the leg, we were a happy crew," remembered Rick. "It was now an easy sail into the harbor."

As *Chessie* neared the finish line, the sea went calm and the breeze quit. George, onboard the tender, began to clap, and Juan's father, onboard the family boat, began to

Spirits were high as *Chessie* raced past its competition. Dave and Rick were all smiles.

FINISH POSITIONS AT LA ROCHELLE

BOAT	OVERALL STANDINGS
Toshiba	478
Silk Cut	560
Chessie Racing	583
EF Education	255
Merit Cup	593
EF Language	744
Swedish Match	629
Innovation Kvaerner	552
Brunel Sunergy	375

yodel his son and the crew to the finish line. Beaming with pride, he explained, "That's the way I used to call Juan for dinner." As the yodeling echoed, Juan climbed out of his nav station and up on deck. With a smile on his face, he waved and yodeled back. Flying the Code 0 whomper, *Chessie* cruised along at 10 knots. "There were lots of smiles on board, and the setting sun cast a beautiful pink glow across the flat water," said Kerry. "It was 10:00 P.M. on May 16."

One question remained: Would *Chessie* make it to La Rochelle before the harbor locks closed? With a 20-foot tidal change, La Rochelle closed its harbor except at high tide. Unfortunately, *Chessie* and the rest of the fleet had missed high tide. They were diverted to a temporary berth in a fishing port, the same port in which the Germans had housed their largest submarine U-boat base during World War II. Now a tourist attrac-

Left: Chessie's crew celebrated their fourth third-place finish with some very tasty French food and wine. Jerry showed his approval. *Bottom:* Lifting the surprised and reluctant navigator, Juan, the crew celebrated their latest success.

tion, the sub pens with the U-boats and the bomb marks are still there.

Dousing each other in champagne, *Chessie*'s crew celebrated their third-place finish and their fourth podium finish. The crew lifted a surprised and reluctant Juan into the air and drenched him in the bubbly. After receiving their medals, the entire crew retired to a hanger and feasted on Brie, páté de fois gras, entrecôte pepper steaks, and, of course, French vin (wine).

After the scores were added up, *Chessie* was in fourth place overall, with a possibility of second or third for the entire race.

La Rochelle, France,

to Southampton, England

LEG

9

DISTANCE
450 nautical miles

START DATE
May 22, 1998

**ESTIMATED
ARRIVAL DATE**
May 24, 1998

La Rochelle, with its narrow, cobblestone streets, church spires, castle towers, and forts, made it easy to imagine knights in shining armor galloping down the streets. Having the Whitbread in town changed the tempo of the city but not the inner clocks, which remained based on the tides. Twice a day, boats lined up to await the opening of the lock gates so they could leave the harbor. Twice a day, they returned. The 20-foot tidal change acted as an anchor for the townspeople.

La Rochelle was full of history. The sea walls had been erected during the tenth century. Then, in the eleventh century, the townspeople dug out the harbor (by hand) and designed the lock system to encourage shipping. By the eighteenth century, after the city had survived numerous attacks and wars, Napoleon commissioned Fort Boyard to be built in the middle of the channel to fire upon attacking ships. By the time the fort was completed, cannon range had increased and it was no longer necessary. Under the city of La Rochelle lies a maze of catacombs,

Through the years, Fort
Boyard has served as a
prison and a private
party destination.
Currently, it is the set
for a globally televised
adventure game.

which the Nazis converted into a bomb shelter
and administration complex during World
War II.

In May 1998, La Rochelle again made
history. For the first time, the Whitbread
Round the World Race had come to France.
La Rochelle opened its gates and welcomed
the fleet with gusto. This would be a short
stopover, but that didn't prevent the parties
and guest appearances. The crew of *EF Education* included two French citizens, Christine Guillou, skipper, and Isabelle Autissier,
the world-famous solo sailor who lived near
La Rochelle, so *EF Education* garnered the
majority of attention, drawing extra large
crowds wherever they went. That didn't,
however, diminish the attention lavished on
the rest of the fleet. The French love offshore
sailing and appreciate world-class sailors. "It
was a great stopover," George and Maureen
agreed. "The people were terrific, and the
food was superb."

EF Language had secured first place, but
five boats—*Swedish Match, Merit Cup, Chessie
Racing, Toshiba,* and *Silk Cut*—still vied for
second and third. *Chessie* had a possibility for
second place and a good chance for third. It
would be a short 450-mile sprint up the
Solent. If everything went as planned, there
would be a photo finish for the fans and the
media.

All the boats received an extra going over.
The wear and tear were showing on the
boats, the crews, and their families. This was
the last leg and, for the majority of the fleet,
the leg that would ultimately decide the race.
In between working on the boat and the
various scheduled appearances, *Chessie*'s crew
members each carved out a little time to
investigate the area. Because there was so
much to see, some of the crew arranged to
return after the race.

For the fourth time, *Chessie*'s crew
mounted the podium. In addition to the

third-place trophy, George received the City of Annapolis Trophy. One of the honors bestowed on *Chessie Racing* was an invitation to the city of Rochefort to see the rebuilding of the frigate *Hermoine,* an exact replica of the boat built in 1779 that took part in the American War for Independence. After a superb dinner and a ceremony commemorating the occasion, the crew toured the facilities and signed *Hermoine*'s keel. Jon Holstrom was in heaven studying their technique. An ambassador for France, like the *Pride of Baltimore,* the *Hermoine* is scheduled to sail to Baltimore.

George had originally planned to sail the final leg, but he pulled himself out of the lineup. "This is our last and only chance. The bottom of the ninth, and we need murderer's row with all the clean-up hitters," George said disappointedly, but competitive to the end. "The best chance for a podium position

overall is with the pros; therefore, I will watch from the boat at the start and get on at the finish as a rail potato."

With the Solent's shoals and tricky waters, *Chessie* decided to enlist Derek Clark, a world-class sailor from the area, for local knowledge. The shortness of the leg allowed for no mistakes; there would be no time for recovery. Whirly would also sit this leg out.

As the boats lined up to leave the harbor, the excitement built to a crescendo. The guest positions were occupied by George and Maureen Collins and Bryan Fishback. Finally, the gates opened, and the sleek, modern W60s paraded through the ancient walls. It was a spectacular sight. Fans packed the harbor, waving and shouting encouragement.

Tooling around near the start line, you could sense the tension. This leg would decide the race outcome. The media was out in force. Some reporters had even hired boats to

Top: The *Hermoine*'s
shell took shape. The
Hermoine measures over
65 meters long, weighs
more than 1,200 tons,
and will carry 1,500
square meters of sail on
three masts.
Left: George added his
signature to the keel.

follow the fleet all the way to Southampton. The Race Committee's planning was paying off. They had orchestrated a media finish, hoping to have the boats competing to the end. With five boats vying for two podium positions, the pressure permeated the fleet.

While seven of the boats took the windward end of the line, *Chessie* and *Merit Cup* were held to the leeward end by the Commit-

tee Boat. Flying her jib top reacher, *Chessie* strategically executed her approach to the start line and then jibed just in front of *Merit.* The start gun misfired, but the nine W60s, relying on the start flag, took off for the first mark. It was up and they were off. *Chessie* beat *Merit* across the line as the massive spectator fleet converged on the racers, churning up big chop. *Merit* suffered. With

CREW FOR CHESSIE RACING

LEG

9

John Kostecki, skipper

Juan Vila, navigator

Grant "Fuzz" Spanhake, watch captain

Dave Scott, watch captain/sailmaker

Jerry Kirby, crew boss/bowman

Gavin Brady, driver

Derek Clark, driver

Rick Deppe, bowman

Greg Gendell, bowman

Antonio "Talpi" Piris, trimmer/driver

Jonathan "Jono" Swain, trimmer/driver

Stu Wilson, grinder/sailmaker

good wind, the other seven boats held high
and bore down for the first mark.

Kerry reported that "*Innovation Kvaerner*
was first to round, followed by *Toshiba, Swedish Match, EF Language,* and *Chessie. EF
Language, Chessie,* and *Silk Cut* chose not to
jibe. It was the right call. Those who did
jibe were faced with the spectator fleet bearing down on them like someone trying to go
the wrong way up a crowded escalator.
Chessie hung on to port jibe the longest, and
it paid big dividends."

The wind played games with the fleet.
One minute it was up; the next it was down.
"At one point, the four leaders had up four
different sail combinations in rapid succession," noted Kerry. *Chessie,* with her new
chute emblazoned with her logo and a
staysail set inside, was on the numbers (right
on course with her sails full). It was a fast sail
combination, and *Chessie* sliced through the
water toward the second mark, a lighthouse
on shallow ground.

Toshiba had Conner back at the helm.
Flying the whomper, she bore down on
Chessie. Hesitating a minute too long, *Chessie*
hoisted her own whomper. By the time the
two boats had reached the second mark,
Toshiba had come abeam of *Chessie.* "Conner
hailed for room—three boat lengths," Kerry
reported. *Chessie* bore away to give them the
room, but *Toshiba* kept coming. *Chessie* jibed
away to prevent a collision and put up her
protest flag. "Conner had taken more room
than he needed," complained John. Although
a tough protest to win, John wanted to send

Top: EF Language and *Chessie* replaced the jibs with their billowing spinnakers.
Left: Chessie's crew worked in unison.

Chessie's chase boat stayed close, ready to pick up the guests.

a message to *Toshiba* that *Chessie* would not tolerate any bullying. Three other protests were lodged during the restart. The battle was definitely heating up.

As the fleet sailed past Île de Re, *Chessie* led. With 30+ knots of wind, it was going to be a long night and a hard leg. *Kvaerner*'s mainsail ripped; she would have to sail with two reefs in the main while the sail was repaired on deck. It was apparent that all the crews would go without sleep and eat on the run. The next 48 hours would be full on. There was little or no time for e-mails. For the duration of the leg, no more than eight miles separated the nine boats.

As the boats rounded Brest, in the northwest corner of France, *Brunel* hugged the coast and picked up a favorable current. *Chessie, Kvaerner,* and *EF Education* sailed farther offshore and went to the back of the standings.

Working her way up and across the English Channel, *Chessie* took the middle route. First the boats to the east made gains; then the boats to the west made gains. *Chessie* was stuck. Disappointed, frustrated, and desperate, the crew searched for wind but found none. "It was Code 0 conditions and the fleet passed us," said a thoroughly frustrated John. "We then made a mistake by putting up a spinnaker, which led us too low on our optimum desired course. The wind went light, and the boats with less current benefited a huge amount. This was the major turning point in the leg. We were never able to recover."

Rick frowned. "We kept looking for an opportunity to recover, but there was not enough runway. We made several sail changes and shifted our weight, but nothing helped." George climbed aboard at Hurst Castle to sail

the remainder of the leg and the race with his crew. "Yeah, we were terribly disappointed," he said, "but those guys were all on my podium. They participated and they competed well throughout the race. I'd sail with them any day."

With a headsail hoisted for the beat up the Southampton River, *Chessie* was locked in eighth place for Leg 9. "It was a terribly disappointing way to finish such an awesome race," sighed John. Rick shook his head as he said, "We were dealt a horrible hand, but that's yacht racing. It wasn't for lack of effort."

As the fleet sailed into Southampton, everyone looked exhausted. Standbridge (*Toshiba*) summed it up by saying, "I've done five Whitbreads, and I've enjoyed them all to varying degrees. I'm not sure how much more stripped out and basic these boats can become; there's nothing in them anyway," he

said. "Any further developments will have to be human ones, sleeping on the rail for instance, no going down below, eating pills instead of food . . . "

Top: **Disappointed and frustrated,** *Chessie*'**s crew sailed across the finish line but not into the harbor.**
Left: **Bowmen Rick and Jerry provided ballast. George climbed on at Hurst Castle to ride the remainder of the race as a rail potato.**

FINISH POSITIONS
AT SOUTHAMPTON

The wives and shore crew went out to meet *Chessie*. The shore crew switched places with the sailors and brought *Chessie* in after the tide came in. Nine months after the start of the race, *Chessie*'s crew returned to South-ampton.

Merit Cup

EF Language

Innovation Kvaerner

Silk Cut

Swedish Match

Toshiba

Brunel Sunergy

Chessie Racing

EF Education

OVERALL POSITIONS

BOAT	STANDING
EF Language	836
Merit Cup	698
Swedish Match	689
Innovation Kvaerner	633
Silk Cut	630
Chessie Racing	613
Toshiba	528
Brunel Sunergy	415
EF Education	275
America's Challenge (dropped out after Leg 1)	48

Chessie took sixth place in the 1997–98 Whitbread Round the World Race, defeating the other two American boats, *Toshiba* and *America's Challenge*. A sixth-place finish was a small consolation, even knowing that the point spread was close.

AMERICA'S CHALLENGE
Nationality: United States
Leg Results: 7 (resigned after Leg 1)
Overall Result: Tenth

The syndicate had a fast boat (one of only two non-Farr boats) and an experienced, successful skipper in Ross Fields. Despite limited preparation, *America's Challenge* carried 11:2 odds. After finishing Leg 1, they discovered that a middleman had run off with the funding. The syndicate had to pull out of the race, and the crew dispersed. The boat was left in Cape Town.

CHESSIE RACING
Nationality: United States
Leg Results: 5, 6, 3, 3, 3, 6, 8, 3, 8
Overall Result: Sixth

Chessie Racing was considered a fast boat with a solid crew. The alternating skipper system hurt her chances. Before the race, her odds were 10:1. *Chessie Racing,* the only nonprofit, privately financed project in the race, had the fleet's smallest budget. The project was led and financed by George Collins.

BRUNEL SUNERGY
Nationality: Netherlands
Leg Results: 10, 9, 8, 8, 2, 8, 1, 9, 7
Overall Result: Eighth

Brunel Sunergy (one of only two non-Farr boats) was considered the slowest of the fleet, probably because of budgetary constraints. It had the second smallest budget. At the beginning of the race, *Brunel Sunergy* carried 20:1 odds. When Roy Heiner took over the role of skipper in Fremantle, he pushed the boat hard and took some gambles, resulting in two podium finishes.

EF EDUCATION
Nationality: Sweden
Leg Results: 9, 8, 9, 9, retired, 9, 9, 4, 9
Overall Results: Ninth

EF Education, the only female team, had strong funding and an experienced crew. The crew's spirit and determination won the hearts and respect of people around the world. Their prerace odds were 50:1. Less upper body strength and multiple equipment breakages prevented them from placing higher in the overall results.

EF LANGUAGE
Nationality: Sweden
Leg Results: 1, 5, 1, 4, 1, 2, 3, 6, 2
Overall Results: First

EF Language had won the Whitbread by Leg 8. Her prerace odds were 16:1, but her whomper sail made for the winning ticket. The only way *EF Language,* with her well-developed whomper and sail development program, could have lost the race would have been by breakages or mistakes. *EF Language* suffered few of either. The syndicate had strong funding, a good solid crew, and a strong support organization.

MERIT CUP
Nationality: Monaco
Leg Results: 2, 7, 4, 1, 5, 5, 6, 5, 1
Overall Result: Second

Sailing his third Whitbread as skipper, Grant Dalton, a dyed-in-the-wool New Zealander, portrayed himself as a rough, tough, and fierce competitor. His crew was made up entirely of New Zealanders. Their prerace odds were 11:4. They scored high and sailed consistently.

INNOVATION KVAERNER
Nationality: Norway
Leg Results: 3, 2, 5, 7, 6, 4, 4, 8, 3
Overall Result: Fourth

Innovation Kvaerner's young team showed great promise. Their prerace odds were 7:1. Knut Frostad, the youngest skipper of the fleet, had sailed with Lawrie Smith in the prior Whitbread. He proved himself quite capable in the role of skipper, and his leadership skills played an important part in building team spirit and determination.

SILK CUT
Nationality: England
Leg Results: 4, 4, 7, 6, retired, 1, 5, 2, 4
Overall Result: Fifth

A prerace favorite, *Silk Cut* began with odds of 7:2. The combination of Lawrie Smith as skipper and strong funding held good promise, but *Silk Cut* didn't produce. In his fourth Whitbread, Smith failed to bring home his long-sought-after prize. *Silk Cut* carried the smallest shore crew, despite its solid budget. A fast boat with a skipper willing to take some chances, *Silk Cut* broke the world's speed record over a 24-hour period—449.1 nautical miles. Its dismasting in Leg 5 prevented it from possibly breaking its own record.

SWEDISH MATCH
Nationality: Sweden
Leg Results: 8, 1, 2, 5, 4, 3, 2, 7, 5
Overall Result: Third

Swedish Match had a solid budget and a strong crew. Her prerace odds were 8:1. Except for Leg 1, she sailed consistently well and fast. The skipper combination of Gunnar Krantz, who had sailed with Lawrie Smith on *Intrum Justicia,* and Erle Williams proved to be quite successful. *Swedish Match* was the only boat that kept the same crew throughout the race. Her crew's professionalism was noted at sea and on shore.

TOSHIBA
Nationality: United States
Leg Results: 6, 3, 6, 2, disqualified, 7, 9, 1, 6
Overall Result: Seventh

One of the prerace favorites with 9:4 odds, *Toshiba* was well funded. Her coskippers, Chris Dickson and Dennis Conner, the only American crew member, were considered two of the best in the world; however, *Toshiba* had problems from the start. After her poor showing in Leg 1, rumors circulated that Chris Dickson would make replacements. Instead, he was replaced. Paul Standbridge had sailed three prior Whitbreads, one with Lawrie Smith. Standbridge was given the responsibility of skipper, but Dennis Conner's presence was always felt. *Toshiba* had the most protests filed against her, two of which (disqualified in Leg 5 and penalized two places in Leg 7) prevented her from placing higher.

GEORGE'S ADVICE TO FUTURE SYNDICATES

- Get a corporate sponsor—you can't win without one.

- Have a two-boat program—the learning curve with a one-boat program is too long.

- Obtain a top-notch sailmaker with W60 Whitbread experience (prior Whitbread experience is not sufficient alone, as maxis competed in prior races).

- Select the skipper and navigator quickly, and let them determine their draft picks for crew.

- Select the crew based on skill and knowledge, carry a few substitutes, and stick with the same crew throughout the race, if possible.

- Arrange for longer on-water training time for W60 knowledge and crew selection.

- Have a fully staffed shore crew so sailors can have minimum shore duty, allowing them to rest when they are in port and concentrate on sailing the boat.

- Settle on equipment, clothing, and food early in the organizational process.

- Impress upon the crew the importance of public relations and ensure its cooperation. With a corporate sponsor, this is critical.

- Schedule more training while in port between legs.

The 1997–98 Whitbread Round the World Race ended with a flourish on May 29, 1998. The boats and crews dispersed around the globe. This would be the last Whitbread Round the World Race; however, the race will continue. It was purchased by Volvo and will continue to be held every four years under its new name, the Volvo Ocean Race. As soon as the awards were presented, preparation for the 2001–2 Volvo Ocean Race began. The route will change a bit, but it will still start in Southampton, England. The 2001–2 race will travel to Cape Town, South Africa; Sydney, Australia (and there participate in the Sydney-Hobart Race); Auckland, New Zealand; Rio de Janeiro, Argentina; Miami and Baltimore/Annapolis, United States; La Rochelle, France; Gothenburg, Germany; and finish in Kiel, Sweden.

During the 1997–98 Whitbread Race, seven collisions with whales were reported, but no serious damage occurred. Flying fish, albatrosses, porpoises, and sharks peppered the crew e-mails. Although there were injuries, all were handled professionally and the victims recovered completely.

Throughout the race and in the months following the race, *Chessie* proved that winning was not everything. In fact, *Chessie* proved to be a huge success. Everyone touched by *Chessie* gained something. The crew sailed one of the most challenging races in the world, competing admirably in a fleet of world-class sailors. The Living Classrooms Foundation gained worldwide recognition. Sailing, as a sport, earned respect and gained numerous new followers in the United States, especially along the Chesapeake Bay. *Chessie* fans enjoyed the adventure of a lifetime and discovered the web. Students around the world learned about academics, sailing, teamwork, and geography. "Yes, *Chessie,* the big green monster from the Chesapeake Bay, won the respect and admiration of everyone

she touched and proved winning isn't everything," Kerry reported to students after the race. "It's all the other stuff that happens when you're trying. And *Chessie* most definitely won in that respect."

The boat, *Chessie Racing,* was sold to the Beau Geste Sailing Team, which sponsors Gavin Brady. The proceeds went to the Living Classrooms Foundation. *Chessie Racing* has been painted a bright red and will serve as the training boat in Beau Geste's bid for the 2001–2 Volvo Ocean Race. Gavin Brady has agreed to coskipper the crew. He will be the youngest skipper in the history of the Whitbread and Volvo Races.

The crew of *Chessie Racing* dispersed.

- **George and Maureen Collins** (Maryland) officially retired; however, they are both still active on numerous charitable boards. George continues to race yachts in major regattas in the United States.

- **Kathy Alexander** (Maryland) is executive director for the Huntington's Disease Society of America—Maryland Chapter.

- **Jim Allsopp** (Maryland) returned to North Sails, where he is director of marketing and product development. He continues to sail on George Collins's race boats.

- **Dave Beiling** (Rhode Island) is working for *Prada,* the Italian America's Cup team, as rigger and boatbuilder.

■ **Gavin Brady** (Maryland), currently ranked second in the World Match Racing Circuit, is forming a syndicate to compete in the 2001–2 Volvo Ocean Race. A number of America's Cup teams are courting him. In his spare time, he sails under the name "Team *Chessie Racing*," sponsored by the Living Classrooms Foundation, and teaches the joys of sailing to some of the students at Living Classrooms.

■ **Rick Deppe** (Maryland) returned to Annapolis with his family. He continues to manage boats for George Collins—a Mumm 30 (*Moxie*), a Santa Cruz 70 (*Chessie Racing*), and a Farr 52 (*Chessie Racing*).

■ **Evan Evans** (Maryland) continues to run his marine electronics business out of Annapolis.

■ **Mark Fischer** (Maryland) returned to manage his advertising and marketing agency, opening a branch office in Park City, Utah.

■ **Stephanie Fischer** (Maryland) is helping Mark open the Park City office and coordinating the renovation of their home in Park City.

■ **Greg Gendell** (Maryland) returned to Annapolis, working for Bank Sails. He has signed on as a member of the John Koius's Aloha Racing team, *Abracadabra,* in the 2000 America's Cup.

■ **Jon Holstrom** (Rhode Island) returned to Goetz Custom Boats for a short time. He has since been hired as boatbuilder for *Prada,* the Italian America's Cup team.

■ **Linda Jones** (Rhode Island) married Dave White, a member of EF's shore crew. They are restoring a home in Newport, Rhode Island, and will be joining the Spanish America's Cup team, *The Spanish Challenge.*

■ **Jerry Kirby** (Rhode Island) returned home to spend time with his family and to manage

his construction company in Newport. He has signed on with *Young America* for the 2000 America's Cup.

■ **John Kostecki** (California) signed on as Paul Cayard's tactician for *AmericaOne* to compete for the 2000 America's Cup. John will skipper the *Pinta Illbruck Round the World Challenge* in the 2001–2 Volvo Ocean Race, using the two EF boats as training boats.

■ **Kurt Lowman** (Maryland) is presently a partner in a telecommunications company located in Bethesda, Maryland.

■ **Jon Patton** (Maryland) enrolled at the Landing School in Kennebunkport, Maine, to study boatbuilding.

■ **Antonio "Talpi" Piris** (Spain) will compete in the America's Cup on the Spanish team, *The Spanish Challenge.*

■ **Tony Rey** (Rhode Island) is currently ranked second on the 1998 U.S. Sailing Team and is working on an Olympic Soling campaign for Sydney 2000.

■ **Rudi Rodriguez, M.D.** (Maryland), works with the Department of Orthopedics of Patuxent Medical Group.

■ **Dave Scott** (Maryland) has returned to North Sails and will be sailing with the Swiss team, *Fast2000,* in the America's Cup.

■ **Sally Scott** (Maryland) has returned to school. In addition, she helps in her son's school, works, and competes in bicycle races.

■ **Rob Slade** (Maryland) continues to build his business—Sport, Speed & Strength—in Baltimore. He was named 1999 NSCA Northeast Conference Strength Coach of the Year and has been recruited to train the U.S. Olympic Sailing Team.

■ **Dee Smith** (California) continues to race on the world circuit.

■ **Grant "Fuzz" Spanhake** (Maryland) consults for North Sails and other sailing projects. He is a sailing team member of Ed Baird's America's Cup team—*Young America.*

■ **Laura Spanhake** (Maryland) is expecting the couple's first child.

■ **Cary Swain** (Maryland) will be the team administrator for Aloha Racing.

■ **Jonathan "Jono" Swain** (Maryland) is a member of the Aloha Racing America's Cup team, *Abracadabra.*

■ **John Thackwray** (Maryland) returned to Annapolis, where he is a marine consultant. George Collins is one of his clients.

■ **Mike Toppa** (Florida) returned to Fort Lauderdale, where he continues to run North Sails Florida. Mike will sail with *Stars and Stripes* in the 2000 America's Cup.

■ **Paul "Whirly" van Dyke** (Connecticut) is currently building Aloha Racing's boats for their America's Cup challenge.

■ **Juan Vila** (Spain) has signed on as navigator for *The Spanish Challenge* America's Cup team and is doing some testing and consulting for *Pinta Illbruck* in their 2001–2 Volvo Ocean Race campaign.

■ **Stu Wilson** (Connecticut) is being actively recruited by a number of America's Cup teams.

■ **The Living Classrooms Foundation** continues to utilize the sailing theme to provide education and job training programs to more than 60,000 children a year.

Postscript

FROM GEORGE COLLINS. Although *Chessie Racing* did not win the race, the boat and crew accomplished their mission. In spite of great odds and many initial setbacks and skepticism, the boat was built. The team organized its program, solved complex logistical problems, selected both shore and sailing crews, stayed true to its goal of keeping a local (Annapolis/Baltimore) and U.S. flavor, represented the children, and drummed up all kinds of grassroots help while racing around the world better than any other U.S. boat. In so doing, *Chessie* brought the premier offshore race—the Whitbread—to the East Coast and the Chesapeake Bay. The boat provided constant communication with the Living Classrooms Foundation and all its followers throughout the race.

The easily recognized lessons were of math, science, ecology, geography, social sciences, and technology. The more complex lessons of the effort should not be forgotten:

To adhere to a sense of purpose, accomplishing its mission by sailing around the world;

To inspire children to take risks—with *Chessie* as the perfect model;

To get children to seek the challenges in life rather than to take the easy road;

To make personal demands on yourself, both physical and mental, through discipline and training;

To share the rewards of life by giving back;

To participate rather than to spectate;

To give the community a team to cheer for and to represent them in a great competition; and

To compete at the highest level against the best the world has to offer.

Some say the rewards sometimes come in the process. Clearly, that was the added attraction here. All the members of the *Chessie Racing* crew stretched and strove beyond their expectations and can lift their heads high for having given their best throughout the race.

Thank you.

FROM MAUREEN COLLINS, JUNE 3, 1998. What an incredible year this has been! Someone likened it to a circus. They were right. Eleven times we set up our containers in the boat villages, and 10 times we took them down. As I write, the containers are being shipped once again.

At times, we were a family of 40 people. We had our sailing crew, our land crew, spouses and children. There was joy, worry, frustration, laughter, and illness. We were introduced to new people, new cultures, and new foods, and we were given a wonderful view of the world through the eyes of the children following *Chessie*. We learned how to use computers and send e-mail. There were the disappointments of losses and the euphoria of four podium finishes.

There was the exhausting travel. Because of side trips to exotic places and trips back to Maryland, Florida, and Connecticut to visit friends and family, I packed and unpacked my own suitcases no less than 46 times and slept in 46 different beds in 11 months (July 1997 through May 1998). Ellen Gammerman, a reporter for the *Baltimore Sun*, asked me (between interviews with George in La Rochelle) how the Whitbread trip was different for me than the way we usually travel. I looked at her and said, "Ellen, normally I would not be found sitting on a rusty beam between two containers and a dipsty Dumpster—in France, no less!" But I didn't get to tell her that normally I would not be out under a starry African sky in a Zodiac searching for a 64-foot boat or be out in Sydney Harbour screaming and cheering *Chessie* to go faster at 2:00 A.M. with a brightly lit Sydney Opera House as a backdrop. And I didn't get to tell her how in normal life I don't drive a race boat out to the start line, as I did in Baltimore and La Rochelle, or "ride the rail" in such a major race. And I didn't get to tell her how, when I am wearing *Chessie* clothes, people stop and talk to me about *Chessie* and the race. And how everywhere we went there were smiling faces. It was magic.

The race is over, and we are left with our memories, photos, clippings, new and old friends. I want to thank all of you who made the trip with us, who visited our ports, sent us e-mail or mail, held our hands, cooked our meals, gave us encouraging words, shared our disappointments, and shared our joy. Thank you for your friendship. It was all magic.

GLOSSARY

Unless noted otherwise, definitions are courtesy of the United States Sailing Association.

Aboard on the boat

Aground a boat whose keel is touching the bottom

Backstay the standing rigging running from the stern to the top of the mast, keeping the mast from falling forward

Ballast weight, usually in the keel of a boat, that provides stability. In a W60, additional ballast is provided by the water ballast system in the hull of the boat.

Batten a thin slat that slides into a pocket in the leech of a sail, helping it hold its shape

Beam the width of a boat at its widest point

Beam reach (point of sail) sailing in a direction at approximately 90 degrees to the wind

Beating a course sailed upwind

Below the area of a boat beneath the deck

Bilge the lowest part of the boat's interior, where water on board will collect

Block a pulley on a boat

Boom the spar extending directly aft from the mast, to which the foot of the mainsail is attached

Boom vang a block-and-tackle system that pulls the boom down to assist sail control

Bottom the underside of the boat

Bow the forward part of the boat

Broach an uncontrolled rounding up into the wind, usually from a downwind point of sail

Broad reach (point of sail) sailing in a direction with the wind at the rear corner of the boat (approximately 135 degrees from the bow)

Bulkhead a wall that runs across the boat from side to side, usually providing structural support to the hull

Buoy a floating marker

Catamaran a twin-hulled sailing vessel with a deck or trampoline between the hulls

Channel a (usually narrow) path in the water, marked by buoys, in which the water is deep enough to sail

Chart a nautical map

Charter to rent a boat

Chop rough, short, steep waves

Cleat a nautical fitting that is used to secure a line

Close-hauled the point of sail that is closest to the wind

Close reach (point of sail) sailing in a direction with the wind forward of the beam (about 70 degrees from the bow)

Cockpit the lower area in which the steering controls and sail controls are located

Companionway the steps leading from the cockpit or deck to the cabin below

Course the direction in which the boat is steered

Crew besides the skipper, anyone on board who helps sail the boat

Current the horizontal movement of water caused by tides, wind, and other forces

Deck the most flat surface area on top of the boat

Desalinator equipment used to take the salt out of salt water (definition supplied by *Chessie Racing*)

Displacement the weight of a boat; therefore, the amount of water it displaces

Dock (1) the structure where a boat may be tied up; (2) the act of bringing the boat to rest alongside the structure

Donkey engine engine used to power the ballast system, desalinator, and electrical system (definition supplied by *Chessie Racing*)

Downwind away from the direction of the wind

Draft the depth of a boat's keel from the water's surface

Ease to let out a line or sail

Fall off bear way, changing course away from the wind

Fast secured

Fetch a course on which a boat can make its destination without having to tack

Fitting a piece of nautical hardware

Foresail a jib or a genoa

Forestay the standing rigging running from the bow to the mast, to which the jib is attached

Forward toward the bow

Foul weather gear water-resistant clothing

Freeboard the height of the hull above the water's surface

Full not luffing

Gear generic term for sailing equipment

Genoa a large jib whose clew extends aft of the mast

Gooseneck the strong fitting that connects the boom to the mast

Grommet a reinforcing metal ring set in a sail

Gust an increase in wind speed for a short duration

Gybe/jibe to change direction of a boat by steering the stern through the wind

Halyard a line used to hoist or lower a sail

Hank a snap hook that is used to connect the luff of a jib onto the forestay

Head (1) the top corner of a sail; (2) the bathroom on a boat; (3) the toilet on a boat

Head down to fall off or bear away, changing course away from the wind

Head up to come up, changing course toward the wind

Header a wind shift that makes your boat head down or sails to be sheeted in

Headsail a jib, genoa, or staysail

Heel the lean of a boat caused by the wind

Helm tiller or wheel that directly controls the rudder

Helmsman the person responsible for steering the boat

High side the windward side of the boat

Hike to position crew members out over the windward rail to help balance the boat by adding ballast

Hull the body of the boat, excluding rig and sails

Hull speed the theoretical maximum speed of a sailboat determined by the length of its waterline

In irons a boat that is head-to-wind, making no forward headway

Jib the small forward sail of a boat attached to the forestay

Jibe/gybe to change direction of a boat by steering the stern through the wind

Jury-rig to improvise a temporary repair

Keel the heavy vertical fin beneath a boat that helps keep it upright and prevents it from slipping sideways in the water

Ketch a two-masted boat with its after mast shorter than its mainmast and located forward of the rudder post

Knockdown a boat heeled so far that one of its spreaders touches the water

Knot one nautical mile per hour

Leech the after edge of a sail

Leeward (LEW-erd) the direction away from the wind (where the wind is blowing to)

Leeward side the side of the boat or sail that is away from the wind

Lifeline plastic-coated wire, supported by stanchions, around the outside of the deck to help prevent crew members from falling overboard

Lift (1) the force that results from air passing by a sail, or water past a keel, that moves the boat forward and sideways; (2) a change in wind direction that lets the boat head up

Line a nautical rope

Low side the leeward side of the boat

Luff (1) the forward edge of a sail; (2) the fluttering of a sail caused by aiming too close to the wind

Lull a decrease in wind speed for a short duration

Magnetic in reference to magnetic north rather than true north

Mainsail (MAIN-sil) the sail hoisted on the mast

Mainsheet the controlling line for the mainsail

Mast the large aluminum or wooden pole in the middle of a boat from which the mainsail is set

Mast step the structure that the bottom of the mast sits on

Masthead the top of the mast

Nautical mile a distance of 6,076 feet, equaling one minute of the earth's latitude

Navigation Rules laws established to prevent collisions on the water

Offshore away from or out of sight of land

Off the wind sailing downwind

On the wind sailing upwind, close-hauled

Outhaul the controlling line attached to the clew of a mainsail, used to tension the foot of the sail

Overpowered a boat that is heeling too far because it has too much sail up for the amount of wind

Overtaking a boat that is catching up to another boat and about to pass it

Points of sail boat directions in relation to wind direction (i.e., close-hauled, beam reaching, broad reaching, and running)

Port (1) the left side of a boat when facing forward; (2) a harbor

Port tack sailing on any point of sail with the wind coming over the port side of the boat

Prevailing wind typical or consistent wind conditions

Puff an increase in wind speed for a short duration

Pulpit a stainless steel guardrail at the bow and stern of some boats

Rail the outer edges of the deck

Rail meat/rail potato sailors providing additional ballast by sitting on the high side of the boat (definition supplied by *Chessie Racing*)

Reach one of several points of sail across the wind

Reef to reduce the size of a sail

Rig (1) the design of a boat's mast(s), standing rigging, and sail plan; (2) to prepare a boat to go sailing

Rigging the wires and lines used to support and control sails

Rudder the underwater fin that is controlled by the tiller or wheel to deflect water and steer the boat

Run (point of sail) sailing with the wind coming directly behind the boat

Running rigging lines and hardware used to control the sails

Shackle a metal fitting at the end of a line used to attach the line to a sail or another fitting

Sheet (1) the line used to control the sail by easing it out or trimming it in; (2) to trim a sail

Shroud standing rigging at the side of the mast

Sked position report (definition supplied by *Chessie Racing*)

Skipper the person in charge of the boat

Slip a parking area for a boat between two docks in a marina

Sloop a single-masted sailboat with mainsail and headsail

Soling open-keel boat; match racing

Southern Ocean a combination of the southern Pacific and Indian Oceans (definition supplied by *Chessie Racing*)

Spar a pole used to attach a sail on a boat

Spinnaker a large billowing headsail used when sailing downwind

Splice the joining of two lines together by interweaving their strands

Spreader a support strut extending across the boat from side to side used to support the mast and guide the shrouds from the top of the mast to the chainplates

Stability a boat's ability to resist tipping (heeling)

Stanchions stainless steel supports at the edge of the deck that hold the lifelines

Standing rigging the permanent rigging (usually wire) of a boat, including the forestay, backstay, and shrouds

Starboard when looking from the stern toward the bow, the right side of the boat

Starboard tack sailing on any point of sail with the wind coming over the starboard side of the boat

Stay a wire support for a mast, part of the standing rigging

Staysail (STAY-sil) a second, small "inner jib," attached between the bow and the mast

Step the area in which the base of the mast fits

Stern the back part of the boat

Stow to store properly

Tack (1) a course on which the wind comes over one side of the boat (i.e., port tack, starboard tack); (2) to change direction by turning the bow through the wind; (3) the lower forward corner of a sail

Tackle a sequence of blocks and line that provides a mechanical advantage

Tail to hold and pull a line from behind a winch

Tide the rise and fall of water level due to the gravitational pull of the sun and moon

Transom the vertical surface of the stern

Trim (1) to pull in on a sheet; (2) how a sail is set relative to the wind

True wind the actual speed and direction of the wind when standing still

Upwind toward the direction of the wind

Vang see **boom vang**

Wake waves caused by a boat moving through the water

Water maker equipment used to take salt out of salt water (definition supplied by *Chessie Racing*)

Waterline the horizontal line on the hull of a boat where the water surface should be

Weather side the side of a boat or a sail closest to the wind

Whomper nickname for Code 0 sail because of the flapping noise it made; an extremely heavy sail that

was measured as a spinnaker but used as a genoa
(definition supplied by *Chessie Racing*)

Winch a deck-mounted drum with a handle offering mechanical advantage, used to trim sheets

Windward toward the wind

Windward side the side of a boat or a sail closest
to the wind

Wing-and-wing sailing downwind with the jib set
on the opposite side of the mainsail

Wipe out total loss of control of a boat (definition
supplied by *Chessie Racing*)

Working sheet the leeward jib sheet that is being
used to trim the jib

INDEX

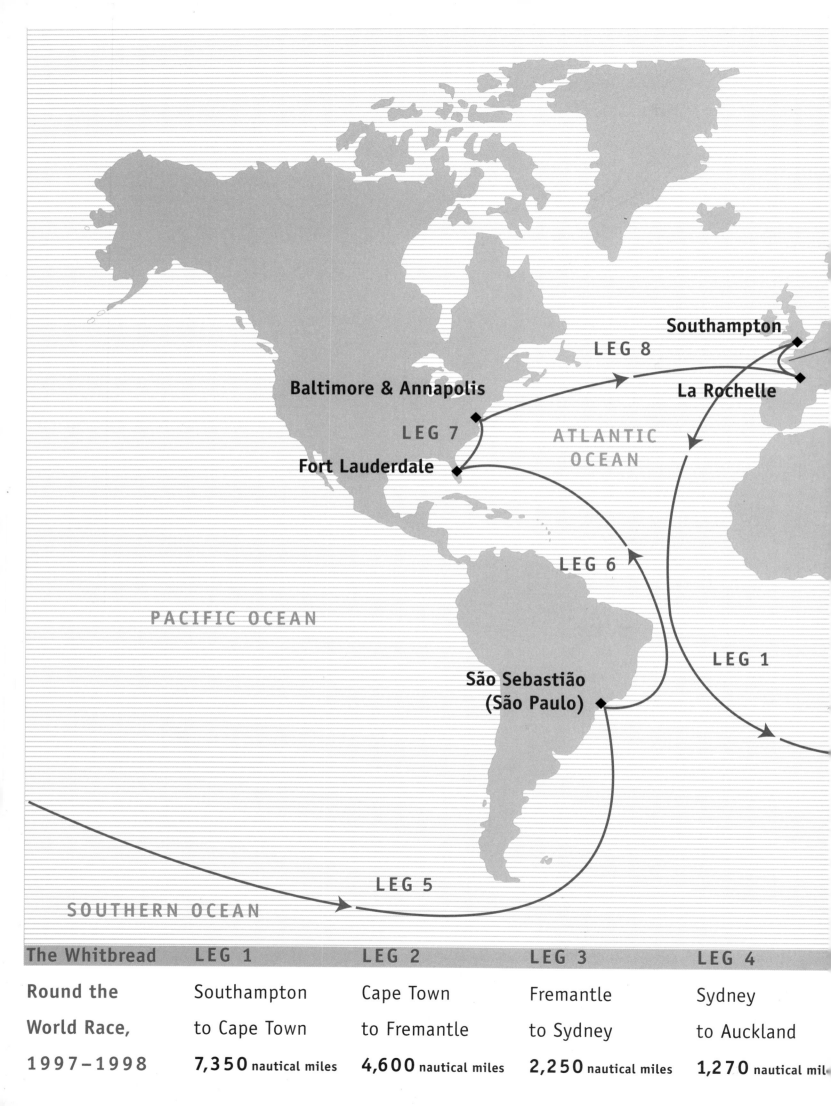

Southampton

LEG 8

Baltimore & Annapolis

La Rochelle

LEG 7

ATLANTIC
OCEAN

Fort Lauderdale

LEG 6

LEG 1

PACIFIC OCEAN

**São Sebastião
(São Paulo)**

LEG 5

SOUTHERN OCEAN

The Whitbread	LEG 1	LEG 2	LEG 3	LEG 4
Round the	Southampton	Cape Town	Fremantle	Sydney
World Race,	to Cape Town	to Fremantle	to Sydney	to Auckland
1997–1998	**7,350** nautical miles	**4,600** nautical miles	**2,250** nautical miles	**1,270** nautical mil